ADAMS AND JEFFERSON

ADAMS
AND
JEFFERSON

A Revolutionary
Dialogue

MERRILL D. PETERSON

OXFORD UNIVERSITY PRESS
OXFORD LONDON NEW YORK

OXFORD UNIVERSITY PRESS
Oxford   London   Glasgow
New York   Toronto   Melbourne   Wellington
Ibadan   Nairobi   Dar es Salaam   Lusaka   Cape Town
Kuala Lumpur   Singapore   Jakarta   Hong Kong   Tokyo
Delhi   Bombay   Calcutta   Madras   Karachi

Library of Congress Cataloging in Publication Data

Peterson, Merrill D
Adams and Jefferson: a revolutionary dialogue.

"Somewhat enlarged version of the Lamar memorial
lectures delivered at Mercer University in October 1975."
Includes bibliographical references and index.
CONTENTS: The American Revolution.—The French
Revolution.—"The revolution of 1800." [etc.]
1. United States—Politics and government—Revolu-
tion, 1775-1783—Addresses, essays, lectures.   2. United
States—Politics and government—1783-1809—Addresses,
essays, lectures.   3. France—History—Revolution—
1789-1799—Addresses, essays, lectures.   4. Adams,
John, Pres. U.S., 1735-1826—Addresses, essays, lec-
tures.   5. Jefferson, Thomas, Pres. U.S., 1743-1826—
Addresses, essays, lectures.   6. Presidents—United
States—Biography—Addresses, essays, lectures.
E210.P47   1978   973.3'092'2   77-13408
ISBN 0-19-502355-2

Printed in the United States of America

FOR MY MOTHER

John Adams: portrait by Mather Brown, 1788
Courtesy of the Boston Athenaeum

Thomas Jefferson's visit with John Adams in London, in 1786, led to a happy exchange of portraits between them. At the urging of Adams and his wife Jefferson agreed to sit for Mather Brown, a young American painter; and the finished portrait soon graced their house on Grosvenor Square. After repeated promptings from Jefferson, Adams reciprocated, sitting for Brown in 1788. When Jefferson received the portrait it was presumably hung at his residence, the hôtel de Langeac, in Paris. Both men received copies of their own portraits as well. John Trumbull, another young American artist abroad, remarked to Jefferson of the two portraits, "Mr. Adams's is like. Yours I do not think so well of." This was the prevailing judgment of the time and present-day students are inclined to agree with it. The likeness of Adams (with Jefferson's *Notes on Virginia* at his side) lacks force and energy, but it is direct and straightforward, unmarred by affectation of any kind. The same cannot be said of Brown's representation of Jefferson, which is dandified, soft, dreamy, and listless. Everyone in Paris, it was said, considered the portrait an *étude*.

Thomas Jefferson: portrait by Mather Brown, 1786
Courtesy of Charles Francis Adams

Contents

Foreword

MERRILL PETERSON'S LECTURES ON ADAMS AND JEFFERSON IN the fall of 1975 continued Mercer University's commemoration of the nation's Bicentennial which began the previous year with Clarence Ver Steeg's lectures in the nineteen-year-old Eugenia Dorothy Blount Lamar Memorial series. This volume contains Professor Peterson's four lectures on "Adams and Jefferson: A Revolutionary Dialogue." Other lectures in the Bicentennial celebration are to be delivered by Professors Jack Greene of Johns Hopkins University (1976) and Richard Beale Davis of the University of Tennessee (1977). A happy relationship exists between Mercer, the sponsoring university, and the University of Georgia Press, the publisher.

Professor Merrill D. Peterson, the Thomas Jefferson Foundation Professor at the University of Virginia, is eminently qualified to interpret the mind and spirit of Jefferson and Adams, two giants of the American Revolution. A native of Kansas and graduate of the University of Kansas, Professor Peterson earned his doctorate at Harvard University. Before his appointment at Virginia he taught at Brandeis and at Princeton. A former Guggenheim Fellow, he has been awarded the Bancroft Prize in American history and the Gold Medal of the Thomas Jefferson Memorial Foundation. He has been a Fellow of the Center for Advanced Study in the Behavioral Sciences at Palo Alto, a Scholar in Residence, Rockefeller Foundation Study Center, Bellagio, Italy, on the faculty at Salzburg Seminar in American Studies, and a Poynter Fellow

at Indiana University. He is a member of the National Historical Publications and Records Commission.

Professor Malcolm Lester of Davidson College, former Dean
of the College of Liberal Arts of Mercer University who earned
his doctorate at "Mr. Jefferson's University," was invited to
participate in the program. In his introduction of the speaker
he emphasized the importance of Professor Peterson's books.
The Jefferson Image in the American Mind (1960) he described as
"a superb study of what history has made of Thomas Jefferson.
It is indeed a notable contribution to the understanding of the
Jefferson symbol in American history." *Thomas Jefferson and the
New Nation: A Biography* (1970), according to Professor Lester,
"by every standard is the best one-volume biography of Jefferson that we have or are likely to have in this generation." These
are only two of the major works by the distinguished scholar.
Numerous works also have appeared under his editorship, the
latest being *The Portable Thomas Jefferson* (1975).

Professor Lester, who was Dean at Mercer at the inception of
the Lamar Memorial Lecture series and who helped influence
Mrs. Walter D. (Eugenia Dorothy Blount) Lamar to make the
substantial bequest which makes possible these lectures, took
the opportunity to review the early history of the program. It
was appropriate, then, for Professor Lester to look back at the
origin of the series which not only brings leading southern
scholars to the Mercer campus each year but also memorializes
the lady who left a handsome legacy to provide "lectures of the
very highest type of scholarship, which will aid in the perma-
nent preservation of the values of Southern culture, history,
and literature." Professor Lester was a willing confederate of
Dr. Spright Dowell, then President of Mercer, and the Honorable William C. Turpin, Mrs. Lamar's attorney, as the three
convinced Mercer's dear friend and neighbor that the University would be a faithful steward of her bequest.

Mrs. Lamar was born in Jones County but grew up in the
Tatnall Square area near Mercer. She attended Wesleyan and

Wellesley Colleges and later was honored with the Doctor of
Laws degree from Mercer. During her lifetime Mrs. Lamar
was a devoted civic and cultural leader in Macon and throughout the South. She gave generously of her time and resources
to her church, to the United Daughters of the Confederacy, to
local dramatic groups, and to projects that furthered the welfare and well-being of her region and people. The Lamar
Lectures are a living tribute to her benevolence and to her
dedicated spirit.

In 1957 President George B. Connell, Dr. Dowell's succes-
sor, instructed Dean Lester to set up the lectureship. His com-
mittee consisted of himself as chairman, Professors Paul
Cousins, Benjamin Griffith, Spencer King, Helen Plymale, and
Henry Warnock. An advisory committee consisted of Dean
John Eidson of the University of Georgia, Mr. Ralph Stephens
of the University of Georgia Press, Mr. Turpin, and Dr. John
Donald Wade of Marshallville, former Professor of Literature
at Vanderbilt and later at the University of Georgia, and
Founding Editor of the *Georgia Review*.

In seeking the advice of Dr. Wade, Professor Lester was told
by that wise and cultured gentleman that institutions like
Mercer "are not only instruments of social change, but are also
the guardians and propagators of the best that has been known
and thought in the world." He urged that "lectures of the
calibre envisioned by Mrs. Lamar should not only be delivered
to appreciative audiences, but should also reach a wider audience of laymen and scholars through publication." To carry
out this purpose, Ralph Stephens of the University of Georgia
Press was consulted. The present Committee echoes the
thought expressed by Professor Lester: "Over the years Mr.
Stephens has rendered an invaluable service in ably directing
the publication of the eighteen volumes of lectures which have
been given."

Large and enthusiastic audiences attended the four lectures
delivered by Professor Peterson under the general theme

"A Revolutionary Dialogue." These lectures treated the dialogue of ideas between Adams and Jefferson, preeminent philosopher-statesmen of "the age of democratic revolution." These giants, so unlike in personality, yet moving together toward a common goal, were friends in 1776, enemies in 1800, and friends again in 1812. Professor Peterson deals with their friendship and their conflicts as he follows their paths, sometimes running concurrently sometimes diverging, and examines their correspondence over the fifty founding years of the young nation. But, as he says, he is concerned also with ideas and events that lay behind and beyond that. Throughout that period they were "at the front of the stage and were constantly seeking out the meaning of the American Revolution."

For those who did not hear the lectures this volume will answer such questions as how and why Adams and Jefferson were friends, and enemies, and friends again; and they will be able to travel those paths with Professor Peterson to the very day when those Revolutionary giants left this world together —on July 4, 1826.

Quoting Professor Lester again: "This subject is in complete accord with the purpose and spirit of the Lamar Lectures, for Adams and Jefferson exemplified that aristocracy of virtue and talent which Eugenia Dorothy Blount Lamar had in mind when she made these lectures possible. To inspire others to enter the aristocracy of virtue and talent was Mrs. Lamar's confident expectation of such scholars as Merrill Peterson."

Spencer B. King, Jr., Chairman
Lamar Memorial Lectures Committee

January 29, 1976

Preface

THIS BOOK IS A SOMEWHAT ENLARGED VERSION OF THE LAMAR
Memorial Lectures delivered at Mercer University in October
1975. A series of lectures is, of course, addressed to a listening
audience, while a book is addressed to a reading audience; and
since there is a difference between listening and reading, it is
never easy to satisfy both audiences with the same production.
The problem begins with the choice of a subject. For the Lamar
Lectures I chose to treat the fifty-year-long relationship between John Adams and Thomas Jefferson—a subject of com-
pelling human interest in itself—as a dialogue of ideas on the
meaning and purpose of the American Revolution. I have long
been concerned with the theme, especially in relation to Jefferson, and welcomed the opportunity to develop it. It seemed to
be manageable in four lectures which might not only hold a
listening audience but also become a readable and instructive
book. I hoped, too, that both lectures and book might make
some small contribution to the nation's observance of its two-
hundredth anniversary.

I want to thank Professor Spencer B. King, Jr., and his
colleagues at Mercer University for the invitation to deliver the
lectures in this distinguished series. Their hospitality made my
visit, and my wife's, a genuine pleasure, and I could not have
asked for a more receptive audience than the one they provided. Thanks are also due to the Rockefeller Foundation and
its Bellagio Study Center, where I was a scholar-in-residence in
the fall of 1974 and where the first draft of the lectures was
written. This was as close as I ever hope to get to nirvana, yet

everything about the Center proved conducive to creative
work. In March 1975 I was on the faculty of the Salzburg
Seminar in American Studies and had an opportunity to try
out my ideas on the fellows from some dozen countries. I am
grateful to them for their patience and their warm response.
Finally, thanks are due to the Research Committee of the
University of Virginia for funds to cover typing of the manuscript and to Mrs. Edith Good for her proficiency in this art.

In quotations from the writings of Adams and Jefferson, I
have generally taken the liberty of modernizing spelling, punc-
tuation, and capitalization.

Merrill D. Peterson

Charlottesville, Virginia
January 30, 1976

ONE

The American Revolution

JOHN ADAMS AND THOMAS JEFFERSON FIRST MET IN JUNE 1775 at the Second Continental Congress in Philadelphia. The Battle of Bunker Hill had just been fought in Adams' Boston. Amidst martial pomp and fanfare Congress dispatched General George Washington to take command of the continental forces rallying near there. Catching the sense of Congress, Jefferson wrote to friends in Virginia that "the war is now heartily entered into, without a prospect of accommodation but thro' the effectual interposition of arms."[1] The war had begun. Incipient revolutionary governments were in being in both Massachusetts and Virginia. But whether American independence would be declared or won, whether the continent would be united, and what the ultimate course of this revolution would be no one could tell. Adams and Jefferson, finding that they thought alike on the great questions before Congress, quickly became friends and coadjutors.

The friendship between them continued, though not without interruption, for half a century, throughout "the age of revolutions and constitutions," as Adams would name it, which he and Jefferson and their compatriots inaugurated in America.[2] The story of their friendship has an appealing human interest, of course, and the later correspondence between them, when they were both retired from the public stage, stands as a literary monument of the age. More important than the story or the correspondence, however, was the dialogue of ideas through which these two philosopher-statesmen carried forward the ongoing search for the meaning and purpose of the American Revolution. The Revolution did not end in 1776 or 1783; it was given a new turn by the French Revolution, and the Jeffersonian "Revolution of 1800" settled its destiny in the American polity. Adams and Jefferson were participants, indeed the chief ideological standard-bearers—at first as political allies, later as political foes—in this entire sweep of democratic revolution. The revolution that had been the basis of the friendship gradually tore it apart, leaving it in tatters in 1800. Yet the friendship was restored in 1812, as partisan and ideological passions receded, mainly through the friendly mediation of Dr. Benjamin Rush. Rush, himself a signer of the Declaration of Independence, seemed to think the reconciliation of these American patriarchs a national responsibility. "I consider you and [Mr. Jefferson] as the North and South Poles of the American Revolution," he told Adams. "Some talked, some wrote, and some fought to promote and establish it, but you and Mr. Jefferson *thought* for us all." [3]

Adams and Jefferson died within hours of each other on the fiftieth anniversary of American independence, July 4, 1826. The full significance of what they had thought, of what they had contributed to the founding of the nation, and, above all, of their reconciliation was thus dramatically enforced on the public mind. Eulogizing the deceased patriots in Boston's Faneuil Hall, Daniel Webster declared, "No two men now live, fellow-citizens, perhaps it may be doubted whether any two men have ever lived, in one age, who, more than those we commemorate, have impressed their own sentiments, in regard to politics and government, on mankind, infused their own opinions more deeply into the opinions of others, or given a more lasting direction to the current of human thought." [4] With the passing of Adams and Jefferson, the curtain fell on the nation's revolutionary age. But, as Webster said, their work and their wisdom had not perished with them. The revolutionary dialogue of fifty years between Adams and Jefferson was an enduring legacy to American liberty.

→»«←

Whatever the later differences between Adams and Jefferson, neither ever doubted "the perfect coincidence" of their principles and politics in 1775–76.[5] Both had risen to positions of revolutionary leadership in their respective provinces. Adams was the veteran of the two. Jefferson was still a young law student in Virginia when Adams, in 1765, made his political debut with the celebrated Instructions of the Town of Braintree, declaring Parliament's Stamp Act unconstitutional. Born in 1735, eight years before Jefferson, he had been longer engaged in the colonial resistance to Great Britain, had served conspicuously in the First Continental Congress, and was widely recognized, along with his cousin Samuel Adams and Patrick Henry and Richard Henry Lee of Virginia, as one of the foremost leaders of the American cause. Thus in the early relationship of the two men Adams was clearly the senior partner. Jefferson deferred to him and would continue to do so for many years. The Virginian's reputation had gone before him to Congress. Since his entrance into the House of Burgesses in 1769, a twenty-six-year-old delegate from western Albemarle County, Jefferson had sided with the party of Henry and Lee and made something of a name for himself as a draftsman of legislative papers championing American rights. His writings were known and admired, Adams later said, for "their peculiar felicity of expression." After a few weeks acquaintance, he noted with approval the judgment of a fellow delegate that Jefferson was "the greatest rubber off of dust" to be met with in Congress—a man of learning and science as well as a forthright politician.[6] In debate on the floor of the House, where Adams excelled, Jefferson seldom uttered a word. The legend grew up, even before they were in their graves, that Jefferson had been "the pen" and Adams "the tongue" (Washington, of course, "the sword") of American independence. "Though a silent member of Congress," Adams recalled, "[Jefferson] was so prompt, frank, explicit, and decisive upon committees and in conversation, not even Samuel Adams was more

so, that he soon seized upon my heart."[7] They saw a good deal
of each other on committees, and Adams said that Jefferson
agreed with him in everything. It is not surprising, then, that
he came to regard Jefferson in the light of a political protégé,
and such was the Virginian's cordiality and esteem that he
returned the favor with every appearance of discipleship.

The course of experience that brought these two men to
Philadelphia in 1775 was in some respects similar. Both were
first sons in the succession of several generations of hardy
independent farmers—Adams at Braintree in the shadow of
Boston, Jefferson in the Virginia up-country where his father
had been among the earliest settlers. However far they strayed,
they always returned to their birthplace as the best place of all,
finally dying there, and for all the honors heaped upon them,
claimed to cherish the title of "farmer" above any other. Both
attended the provincial college—Harvard in Massachusetts,
William and Mary in Virginia—and then prepared for the bar.
Beginning with the *Institutes* of Lord Coke, the Whig champion
against the Stuart kings, they mastered the entire history of
English law, which provided the foundation of their political
opinions. Both men made their provincial reputation at the
bar; they were practicing lawyers before they were politicians,
but as the Revolution came on they were forced to abandon
their profession and neither ever really returned to it.

Adams and Jefferson were preeminently students, not only
of law but of history and philosophy and literature, both ancient and modern. They were avid readers—and readers with
a purpose. Fragmentary notes on what they read appear in
their surviving "commonplace books." While their personal
tastes varied, many of the same names—Cicero, Sidney, Locke,
Bolingbroke, Montesquieu, Hutcheson, Hume—turn up in
the early reports of their reading. If Jefferson was more con-
sciously a student of the Enlightenment, exalting nature and
reason against mystery and authority, Adams also felt its
liberating influence. A youthful ambition of both men was to

build a large personal library. And they succeeded, after considerable effort and financial sacrifice. Jefferson's library numbered over six thousand volumes when it was sold to Congress in 1815, becoming the nucleus of the Library of Congress; and Adams' collection, while only half as large at the time of his death (it was left to the Boston Public Library) was perhaps not much behind Jefferson's when at its fullest.[8] Being studious men in love with their books, their families, and their firesides, both were rather reluctant politicians. For several years after the Stamp Act controversy, Adams wavered between Boston and Braintree, repeatedly forswore the noisy political world of Sam Adams for the quiet, along with the fortune, of his profession, and only finally surrendered himself to the revolutionary movement in 1773. Jefferson, although he grew up in a society where government was the responsibility of the class to which he belonged, experienced the same ambivalence and, unlike Adams, never overcame it.

These similarities of background and interest were undoubtedly important in laying the basis of friendship; more important in the longer run of history, however, were differences of temperament, of intellectual style and outlook, of social and political experience, which were less apparent in 1775 than they would be fifteen or twenty years later. Adams was a latter-day son of New England Puritanism. Although he shook off the theological inheritance from the fathers, he cherished the Puritan past and rather than replace the original model of a Christian commonwealth—John Winthrop's "city upon a hill"—he sought to transform it into a model of virtuous republicanism. The Puritans had come to Massachusetts Bay to worship as *they* pleased, and however noble their ideal it was not an ideal of religious or political freedom. Yet in his first published essay, *A Dissertation on the Canon and Feudal Law*, 1765, Adams reconstructed the Puritan past into a legend of republican beginnings, thereby conscripting it in the cause of revolution. "It was not religion alone, as is commonly supposed, but it was a love of universal liberty . . . ," he wrote, "that projected, conducted, and accomplished the settlement of America."[9] The fundamental institutions established by the Puritans—congregations, schools, militia, and town meetings —must remain the pillars of the community, and no government, republican or whatever, could survive unless it was ordered on "the perfect plan of divine and moral government."[10] The duties of religion being the only sure foundation of public virtue and happiness were an obligation of the state. The strain of Calvinism, which thus entered into Adams' republican vision, colored his theory of human nature. "Sin," although wrenched from its old theological associations, remained a prominent word in his political vocabulary, roughly translated as human weakness and selfishness. Reading Montesquieu through Calvinist lenses, Adams deemed austerity of morals and manners indispensable to republican government. "But," he said in 1776, "there is so much rascality, so much venality and corruption, so much avarice and ambition . . . among all ranks and degrees of men even in America, that I sometimes doubt whether there is public virtue enough to support a republic."[11] He was a doubting republican at the starting gate, one for whom the American Revolution carried the heavy burden, added to everything else, of moral regeneration after the old Puritan vision.

Now to all this Jefferson, virtually untouched by the Puritan dispensation, presents a sharp contrast. Virginia had no legend of pure and noble beginnings, nothing peculiarly edifying in its past, no glorious heritage to preserve. And to be a revolutionary there was to be an enemy, if not of religion, then of the established Anglican Church which dominated the landscape. Unlike Adams, for whom the New England church was an ally, Jefferson came to the Revolution as a man alienated from the traditional religious culture of his community. Taking his moral and political directives from the modern philosophy of the Enlightenment, Jefferson felt no need to maintain the centrality of religion in human affairs. Indeed it was one of the missions of the Enlightenment to retire God to the wings and place man at the center of the stage. Destiny was no longer controlled by Providence but by Nature. Man was inherently good, seeking his own happiness through the happiness of others, and with the progress of knowledge Nature would answer all his purposes. Civil education was required, but not churchly discipline. Religious restraints, even the hope of Heaven and the fear of hell, were unnecessary; in so far as they were supported by civil government they were unjust. Just as morality had no certain dependence on religion, religion was of no concern to the state. As Jefferson would write in the Virginia Statute for Religious Freedom, "our civil rights have no dependence on our religious opinions, more than our opinions in physics or geometry." [12] With this view Adams could not agree. For him the American Revolution was a continuation under new auspices of an old quest for a pure and righteous commonwealth, while for Jefferson it looked to the liberation of the individual from all conceptions of higher moral authority embodied in church or state.

The friendship between Adams and Jefferson was a triumph of will over seeming incompatibilities of personal temperament and intellectual style. Neither man, one short and stout, the other tall and lean, could have seen himself reflected in the other. Adams was warm and contentious, Jefferson cool and agreeable. Adams was impulsive and careless, Jefferson deliberate and precise. Adams was a gyroscope of shifting moods; his nerves, as Mercy Warren once told him, were "not always wound up by the same key." [13] Jefferson's nerves, together with the compass of his mind, were amazingly steady. Adams always wore his heart on his sleeve and perceived the world about him as a drama in which he was the central character. Jefferson, while not an insensitive man, approached the world through his reason and concealed his inner feelings behind an almost impenetrable wall of reserve. Adams, by his own confession,

was "a morose and surly politician."[14] Jefferson, if seldom a
happy politician, proved amiable and sanguine. He was more
impressed by the scope than by the limits of human possibilities. "My temperament is sanguine," he would later tell Adams.
"I steer my bark with Hope in the head, leaving Fear astern."
And if he did not classify the New Englander with "gloomy and
hypochondriac minds" always full of foreboding, it would
nevertheless sometimes be a fair description of his friend's
outlook.[15] Finding himself awkward and churlish in social
intercourse, Adams supposed the fault lay in the New England
character, which he contrasted with "the art and address" of
the southern gentlemen he met in Congress.[16] Jefferson, of
course, while not at all typical of the southern breed, possessed
"art and address" in abundance, including those qualities of
subtlety, grace, and refinement so conspicuously lacking in
Adams. A friend of his youth remarked that he had "a little
capillary vein of satire" meandering about in his soul which was
as powerful as it was sudden.[17] This Swiftian mode did not suit
Jefferson. He disapproved of satire and hid what little humor
he had under "the pale cast of thought." What was ludicrous in
life was cause for regret rather than amusement. Expecting so
much of men, and nations too, he could not laugh at their
follies, least of all at his own. To Jefferson's lofty idealism his
friend opposed an obsessive realism, alternately stern or satiric
as befit his mood. While there was something endearing in
Adams' robust honesty—and Jefferson found it—it inevitably
offended men with feelings scarcely less tender than his own
and contributed to that unpopularity of which he would constantly complain.

The New Englander was, basically, an insecure person. His
yearnings for fame, his notorious vanity and airs of conceit,
grew from massive layers of self-doubt. In early manhood
(occasionally afterwards) he kept a diary—another mark of his
Puritan heritage—which was filled with upbraidings, self-
catechizing questions, and self-improving resolutions. As late

as his thirty-seventh year of age, he could admonish himself, "Beware of idleness, luxury, and all vanity, folly, and vice!" Half his life had run out, and what a poor, insignificant atom he was! "Reputation," he often told himself, "ought to be the perpetual subject of my thoughts, and aim of my behavior." [18] At last, with the onrush of revolution, he resolved to pursue reputation by power rather than by fortune. He found, as did Jefferson, new scope for his abilities. But even at the height of political achievement, he was plagued by anxieties. "I begin to suspect that I have not much of the grand in my composition," he confided to his ever-understanding wife Abigail in 1777.[19] Then and later he felt his services and sacrifices were unappreciated. "I have a very tender, feeling heart," he wrote. "The country knows not, and never can know, the torments I have endured for its sake." [20] In time, he became morbid on the subject. Jefferson was rarely afflicted in this way. He was an Epicurean, though of sober mien, to whom emotional torment and self-flagellation were alien. Never in his life did he keep a personal diary. He kept records of everything—gardens, the weather, Indian languages—except the state of his soul. His self-possession, his easy, almost bland, sense of personal security left little room for inner questioning. Unlike the Yankee commoner, he did not have to scratch or fight his way to power. The road had been blazed for him by his father; in a sense, it went with his social position. He could, therefore, feel relaxed about it. Although endowed with a normal amount of ambition, it never became an obsession. Political power in itself held no charms for him. He often said that nature had destined him for the tranquil pursuits of the arts and sciences. None of the heroes of his early life, certainly not the Enlightenment trinity of Bacon, Newton, and Locke, was associated with political power. If that were taken away from him, it would have caused Jefferson no regrets, in fact would have afforded a welcome release to his talents in other and, he thought, better directions. Adams, who committed himself fully to the career and the fame of a founding father, had no such reserves to fall back on.

The fact that one man came to the Revolution through Massachusetts politics, the other in Virginia, also made a difference. For Adams the torch had been ignited by James Otis' constitutional argument against the writs of assistance in 1761, while for Jefferson it was Patrick Henry's celebrated speech against the Stamp Act that had set "the ball of revolution" in motion. The true cause of the Revolution in Massachusetts, Adams believed, was "the conspiracy against liberty" hatched at the conclusion of the Great War by the local "court party" of Governor Francis Bernard, Thomas Hutchinson, and the brothers Andrew and Peter Oliver. It was this junto of high officials, not king and Parliament, that first plotted to tax Massachusetts with the base aim of increasing their own fortunes, securing their independence of the legislature, and establishing a local oligarchy. The enemy, then, was less the British government abroad than it was a corrupt Tory party at home. As late as 1775, Adams fixed the blame for British errors on the colonial Tories.[21] This vivid sense of an internal struggle between "court" and "country" parties—one that threw Adams back into the political world of Walpole and Bolingbroke—was lacking in Virginia. There no Tory party threatened; notwithstanding factional quarrels at Williamsburg, the gentry stuck together, as they always had, and ruled without challenge except from the mother country. In Jefferson's mind, certainly, Britain was the culprit and no residue of affection, such as Adams would continue to feel, remained in him after 1776. Moreover, the popular agitation which radical Whigs used to stoke the revolutionary furnace in Massachusetts raised in Adams fears of upheaval from below such as were scarcely felt in Virginia. There the patricians, secure in their power, not only began the Revolution but ended it. Against the popular torrent Adams bravely defended Captain Thomas Preston and the British soldiers accused of murder in the Boston Massacre.

He was wary of the "mischievous democratic principles" of cousin Samuel and warned repeatedly against the "rage for innovation." [22] Years later he wondered if he should not repent for the "firebrands" he had himself thrown into the flames from 1765 forward. [23] Jefferson expressed no such fears. On the contrary, he thought Virginia could use a little of the "leveling spirit." And the southern aristocrat went on to become the legendary apostle of democracy, while the northern bourgeois acquired the reputation of an apologist for order and hierarchy. Finally, because the war began in Massachusetts and the resources of the continent were wanted for her defense, Adams sought a strong confederation melting the states "like separate parcels of metal, into one common mass," while Jefferson, with other Virginians and the great majority of Congress, saw neither the urgency nor the wisdom of this. [24] As the war progressed, Adams changed his mind, only to return to his earlier opinion a decade later.

Whatever may have been the cause of the American Revolution, the major issue in debate was the constitutional authority of Great Britain over the colonies. As Whigs of a more or less radical stamp, Adams and Jefferson tended to think alike on the issue and, barring small details, reached the same conclusions. What they sought in 1775 and earlier was not independence but reconciliation on the terms of the British constitution; yet as their theory of the constitution was in direct conflict with the regnant theory in Britain, the arguments they advanced unraveled the imperial relationship, forcing the ultimate choice of submission or independence. Jefferson addressed the issue in *A Summary View of the Rights of British America*, published in 1774, while Adams' most labored constitutional argument appeared in the *Novanglus* essays of 1774–75. [25]

The polemics offered two versions of the same theory of the empire and of American rights within it. From the beginning of the contest with the mother country, the Americans had attempted to find some halfway house between total submission to the authority of Parliament, which British opinion demanded, and its total rejection. Generally, the line had been drawn between *external* and *internal* legislation, Parliament having authority in one sphere, as in the regulation of trade, but not in the other. Any line offered difficulties in theory as well as in practice, however. Since they were not represented in Parliament, the colonists claimed that it could not legislate for them, and the tradition of the English constitution lent support to the claim. But the new Whig theory of parliamentary supremacy, stemming from the Revolution of 1688, buttressed by the conventional political wisdom that rejected any idea of two sovereign authorities in the same state—the specter of *imperium in imperio*—proved troublesome for the Americans. Jefferson and Adams, therefore, repudiated the authority of Parliament altogether and set forth a new theory of the empire as a commonwealth of equal self-governing states owing allegiance to a common king. Jefferson reached this position by way of the argument that the Americans were the sons of expatriated men who had possessed the *natural* right "of going in quest of new habitations, and of there establishing new societies, under such laws and regulations as to them shall seem most likely to promote public happiness." This right being natural, the colonists were as free as if they had returned to a state of nature; but, said Jefferson, they voluntarily chose to submit themselves to the British monarch, "who was thereby made the central link connecting the several parts of the empire thus newly multiplied." [26] Adams' reasoning was similar. America was a discovered, not a conquered, country; the first settlers had a natural right, which they exercised, to set up their own governments and enact their own laws consistent with their obligations to the king. These obligations, in the Massachusetts case, were contained in a royal charter, a *compact* with the king. Partly because of the crucial role of this compact in the history of Massachusetts, for which there was no equivalent in Virginia, Adams' argument was more historical and legalistic than Jefferson's. But both appealed to the past in the defense of rights that were basically moral and, in the final analysis, could only be justified on the law of nature.

The advanced position staked out by these writings, adopted in spirit though not in form by Congress, placed the responsibility for reconciliation on the shoulders of George III. He alone held the scepter of the empire. The *Summary View* ended with an appeal to his justice: "No longer persevere in sacrificing the rights of one part of the empire to the inordinate desires of another, but deal out to all equal and impartial right."[27] The anomaly of American Whigs appealing from Parliament to the king did not go unnoticed. "Their language . . . was that of Toryism," Lord North sneered.[28] George III was himself too good a Whig to side with the Americans against Parliament. Their "humble petitions" were answered with muskets and cannon.

It is difficult to say just when Adams and Jefferson gave up the hope of reconciliation and became advocates of independence. For several months after the fighting began both supported armed resistance as a means of bringing Britain to her senses and winning a settlement on American terms. But Britain proved incorrigible. Adams later claimed that he was the constant advocate of independence from the reassembling of Congress after the August recess of 1775. Yet in January of the new year he said that independence was "utterly against my inclinations" and a few weeks later stated his position as "reconciliation if practicable and peace if attainable," quickly adding that he thought both impossible.[29] Jefferson's posture was much the same. Reconciliation was his desire, but rather than submit to British pretensions to legislate for America he would "sink the whole island in the ocean."[30] Neither man, it seems fair to say, rushed into independence, but both were willing to risk it and, further, to demand it if resistance within the empire failed of solution. There were sound political reasons for soft-

pedaling independence in the winter of 1775–76. The delegates of the middle colonies, in particular, were firmly opposed
to the ultimate step, to which they believed the Massachusetts
brace of Adams covertly aimed. Independence could not be
declared until a public opinion had been created for it up and
down the continent. This was the work of Thomas Paine's
Common Sense early in the new year. With a popular political
rhetoric neither Adams nor Jefferson commanded, Paine
transformed independence from a frightful bugaboo to a cap-
tivating vision. In the puffery of his old age, Adams denigrated
Paine, saying that *Common Sense* was a mere distillation of his
own speeches in Congress for the preceding nine months.[31]
Jefferson knew better and always praised Paine's service to the
cause.

"Every post and every day rolls in upon us," Adams rejoiced
in May, "Independence like a torrent."[32] His principal concern
at this time was for the establishment of new constitutional
governments in all the colonies, which would make independence a *fait accompli* and also ensure the maintenance of civil
order. Congress finally passed his and Lee's resolution for this
purpose—"a machine to fabricate independence"—on May
15. Three weeks later it debated the Virginia resolution calling
upon Congress to declare the thirteen colonies free and independent states. Although the vote was postponed, a five-man
committee was appointed to prepare a declaration of independence. Rather surprisingly, Jefferson found himself named at
the head of the committee whose leading members were Benjamin Franklin and Adams. Jefferson's later testimony was that
the committee asked him to draft the proposed paper. Adams,
on the other hand, remembered a conversation in which Jefferson tried to persuade him to do it. He demurred for three
reasons: "Reason first—You are a Virginian, and a Virginian
ought to appear at the head of this business. Reason second—I
am obnoxious, suspected, and unpopular. You are very much
otherwise. Reason third—You can write ten times better than I

can."[33] If the conversation actually occurred, Adams later found reason to regret his decision. In time the authorship of the Declaration of Independence gave Jefferson an éclat with the public that all of Adams' revolutionary services could not match, and he resented it.

But supposing Adams had written the Declaration of Independence, would it have been a very different document? In point of style, it would surely have been less elevated but perhaps more vigorous, less mannered and more natural, less trim and direct and more long-winded. The body of the work, with its bill of particulars against the king, would have been similar because these charges had been more or less codified by Congress during the preceding months. It seems unlikely, however, that Adams would have, or could have, duplicated Jefferson's feat in the preamble. In a document intended to justify the colonies' separation from Great Britain, Jefferson seized the occasion to advance in axiomatic terms a political philosophy for the new nation. Capsuling the principles in electrifying phrases—"all men are created equal," "unalienable rights . . . life, liberty and the pursuit of happiness," "the consent of the governed"—he gave the Revolution a sense of direction at once moral and political and raised the American cause above parochialism, above history, by uniting it with the cause of mankind. This was a triumph. Not that there was anything original in this philosophy of liberty; as Jefferson himself said years afterwards, when it became fashionable in some quarters, even at the Adams homestead, to belittle the Declaration as a hackneyed performance, he had aimed not to discover new principles or to say new things but "to place before mankind the common sense of the subject."[34] It was Adams' "common sense" too, of course. But what was so remarkable about Jefferson's achievement was the ease and completeness with which he transcended the older historical and legal defenses and embraced the rationalism and universalism of the natural rights philosophy, thereby associating the

American Revolution with the aspirations of the Enlightenment. Adams, with a mind more closely bound to the past,
could not have made this leap into the future.

Jefferson showed both Adams and Franklin a rough draft of
the Declaration, and neither had much to suggest in the way of
changes. From the committee the final draft went to Congress
on June 28. There, after voting the Virginia resolution for
independence on July 2, the delegates debated Jefferson's
handiwork for two and one-half days. Many changes were
made, nearly all of them for the worse in his opinion. He was
especially incensed by the elimination of the angry paragraph
indicting the king for waging "cruel war against human nature
itself" by forcing on the colonies the traffic in African slaves.
Adams doubtless supported his friend on this question, as on
every other. He was "the colossus" in the debate, Jefferson later
said, the Declaration's "pillar of support on the floor of Congress, its ablest advocate and defender against the multifarious
assaults it encountered." And even after some of Adams' as-
persions on the document came to public notice decades later,
Jefferson generously praised "the zeal and ability" with which
he had fought for "every word" of it in Congress.[35] Oddly
enough, neither man sent up any huzzahs upon the adoption
of the Declaration of Independence. Adams thought the
landmark decision had been taken earlier, on July 2. That was
the crucial action; Jefferson's paper only declared it. He wrote
to Abigail: "The second day of July, 1776, will be the most
memorable epocha in the history of America. I am apt to
believe it will be celebrated by succeeding generations as the
great anniversary festival. It ought to be commemorated, as
the day of deliverance, by solemn acts of devotion to God
Almighty. It ought to be solemnized with pomp and parade . . .
from one end of the continent to the other, from this time
forward, forevermore."[36] He prophesied the celebrity of
American independence with future generations but was off
the mark as to the anniversary date. Obviously, neither he nor

Jefferson fully appreciated in 1776 the power of words, great words, to symbolize action and to become its monument.

For several months the two congressmen had been turning their thoughts to the creation of new governments in the colony-states. The uncertainty on what new governments would succeed the old could be viewed as an obstacle to independence or, as by Adams and Jefferson, a glorious opportunity. It was, the former declared, "a time when the greatest lawgivers of antiquity would have wished to live. How few of the human race have ever enjoyed an opportunity of making an election of government—more than of air, soil, or climate—for themselves or their children!"[37] Jefferson also felt the challenge. The creation of new government, he said, "is the whole object of the present controversy."[38] But no one responded more eagerly or more soberly to the challenge than Adams. Months before independence was declared he had been calling for the formation of new governments. All the books he had read on the theory and practice of government now found immediate application, and he went back to reread them. There was no more agreeable employment than researches "after the best form of government," he said. Politics was "the divine science"—"the first in importance"—and, while centuries behind most other sciences, he hoped that in this ripening "age of political experiments" it would overtake the rest.[39] When several southern delegates came to Adams in the early months of 1776 seeking advice on the planning of new state governments, he wrote out his ideas in a brief epistolary essay which was so much admired by those who saw it that he consented to its publication, anonymously, under the title *Thoughts on Government, in a Letter from a Gentleman to his Friend*.[40] Adams later said that the letter was written to counteract the plan of government loosely advanced by that "disastrous meteor" Thomas Paine, in *Common Sense*. Paine's crude and half-lettered ideas, got up to please the popular party in Pennsylvania and taken up by no less a personage than Benjamin Franklin, threatened much harm, in Adams' opinion. The plan was "too democratical," mainly because it concentrated all power in a single representative assembly. It was also too simple, for Paine supposed that in government as in nature the simpler anything is the less likely is it to get out of order. Adams, on the contrary, drawing upon a tradition tracing back through Machiavelli to Aristotle, made it an axiom of his political science that all simple government, whether monarchy, aristocracy, or democracy, is bad, and complex government, mixing and balancing opposing principles, is good.

In the *Thoughts on Government* Adams began by insisting, against Alexander Pope, on the importance of the *form* of government, then went on to show that the *republican* form is the best. Borrowing from Montesquieu's theory on the unique spirit appropriate to the different forms of government, agreeing that the spirit of republics is *virtue* (selfless devotion to the commonweal), Adams reasoned that since the practice of virtue produces the greatest happiness to the greatest number of people, a republic is the best form of government. A virtuous people makes a republic possible; its survival makes the cultivation of virtue necessary. But what is a republic? Adams always had trouble defining it. It is "an empire of laws, and not of men," he said. But this described the principle of constitutionalism, not the form of government, and implied that a government of unjust laws, laws against natural right, might be republican. At other times Adams said a republic is a government in which the people have "an essential share" in the sovereign power.[41] Nearly all the American Whigs in 1776 favored republican government, perhaps not unlike the governments they were used to but with written constitutions and the vices of monarchy eliminated. The issue was how popular, how democratic, these new republics should be. And here Adams, as compared to Paine, or even Jefferson, took a moderate position. In his view, and by either of his definitions, the British government was a type of republic, one in which the three pure forms, monarchy, aristocracy, and democracy, were ingeniously balanced in king, lords, and commons. Like most colonial Americans and most enlightened Europeans, Adams had been taught to admire that "most stupendous fabric of human invention," the British constitution, but unlike Jefferson and so many others whose admiration sank in the decade before the Revolution, Adams venerated it to the end of his days as "a masterpiece."[42] Unfortunately, it was not made for the government of colonies; independence came about because the Americans were denied the most valuable part of the constitution, democratic representation.

Holding these views, Adams experienced some difficulty formulating a conception of American republicanism detached from the British model. He was not alone in this; certain categories and dogmas of the British constitution survived in Jefferson's mind too. But for Adams the problem increased rather than lessened after 1776; and compared to his mature political theory, *Thoughts on Government* was a democratic document. It followed from the definition of a republic that the constitution should be so contrived as to secure an impartial "government of laws." The representative assembly should be an exact portrait in miniature of the interests among the people at large. Because of the wide distribution of property in America, at least in New England, this would ensure substantial democracy. But no government in a single assembly could long preserve the freedom and happiness of the people. Absolute power, from whatever source derived, must inevitably grow corrupt and tyrannical. And so Adams called for an upper house to check the lower and a first magistrate with an unqualified negative on the legislature. He also called for an independent judiciary, rotation in office, annual elections, and so on, which were the clichés of old Whig political science.

Jefferson could cheerfully endorse most of what Adams recommended. The differences between them at this time did not fundamentally concern the form or structure of government but the extent of the government's commitment to the ideals of freedom and equality declared in the country's birthright. On balance, Adams was more interested in restoring order than in promoting reform. He eschewed radical experiments, such as Pennsylvania's, and wished the Americans might glide as insensibly as possible into lawful governments. Generally, his plan conformed to the better colonial models, such as that of Massachusetts, and it left the society unchanged. Even as he advocated republican government, he was beset by fears for its success from the want of virtue in the people. America had more of it than other nations, and New England more of it than the rest of America, yet this new people, for all the blessings of Divine Providence, was not exempted from the common vices of humanity. There was so much littleness and selfishness, so much disrespect for rank and status, so much luxury and avarice and talent for political corruption, even in New England, that wise and honest men might soon look to the security of a monarch. To his good friend Mercy Warren he confessed, "I sometimes tremble to think that, although we are engaged in the best cause that ever employed the human heart, yet the prospect of success is doubtful not for the want of power or of wisdom but of virtue." [43]

Jefferson had a more consoling philosophy for a republican, one which assumed the virtue of the people from an innate moral sense in every man and diminished the role of the state in the regulation of human affairs. With his image of a naturally beneficent and harmonious society, an image derived from philosophy rather than experience, government simply did not have for him the preeminent importance Adams assigned to it. Its primary purpose was to secure individuals in their natural rights and thereby to liberate them for action in society. In Jefferson's view government should be absorbed into society, becoming truly self-government, while Adams believed that society must be absorbed into government, reproduced in it, and regulated by it. Theories of human nature

help to explain the difference. Adams, although he thought
Machiavelli, Hobbes, and Mandeville had painted human nature too black, without any color of benevolence, nevertheless
felt that "self-love" was the dominant passion in men and that
government must deal with it. Jefferson, in opposition to these
philosophers, believed that the moral sense, in which all men
were equal, naturally led them to seek the good of others and to
live justly in society.[44] He regarded man primarily as a social
animal, naturally made for society; Adams regarded man as a
political animal, constantly competing for power and therefore, in Paine's metaphor, but beyond Paine's reasoning, re-
quiring government as "the badge of his lost innocence." Simi-
larly, in their attitudes toward history, Adams found political
wisdom in the past and thought that the future, whatever its
advances, would repeat the experience of the past, while for
Jefferson the past was the habitation of specters to be vanquished by reason. History was valuable chiefly for its admoni-
tions, and he became an authentic spokesman of the progressive hopes of the Enlightenment. The future was written in
nature, not in history.

Both men framed constitutions for their native states. When
he was in Congress in the spring of 1776, Jefferson drafted a
fundamental law for Virginia and forwarded it to the revolutionary convention meeting in Williamsburg.[45] It arrived too
late for serious consideration, however; and had it arrived
earlier, Jefferson's plan might not have received that consideration, for it was widely at variance with the conservative constitution adopted for Virginia. Except that it stripped away all
semblance of monarchical power, the new government was like
the old. It did not in any way alter the distribution of power in
Virginia society. It continued the freehold suffrage qualification under which one-third or more of the adult white males
were disenfranchised, the unequal system of representation
which favored the East over the West—"old" Virginia over
"new" Virginia—and it consolidated the oligarchical power of

the local authorities, the county courts. Influenced in part by Adams' *Thoughts on Government*, the Virginia Constitution was an instrument neither of democracy nor of reform.

Jefferson's plan also contained conservative features. He was as eager as Adams, for instance, to divide the legislative power and to secure through an upper house, or senate, a kind of aristocratic check on the annually elected popular assembly. But he had difficulty finding a logical basis for differentiating the two houses of a consistently republican legislature. He had at first thought of life appointment of senators, then quickly rejected it, as he also rejected the solution that would be adopted in several of the new state constitutions of founding the lower house on numbers (population) and the upper on property. Finally, he decided on election of the senators by the popular body for staggered terms of nine years, yet was unhappy with this solution. The English theory of balanced government hung in his mind, a ruin from the past, for which he could find no satisfactory place in the political creed of the Revolution. But Jefferson, unlike Adams, gradually got rid of intellectual survivals such as this one as he matured a democratic philosophy of government.

In accordance with that philosophy, still inchoate in 1776, Jefferson proposed in his draft constitution to extend the suffrage to all taxpayers, thus beginning the breakdown of the centuries-old freehold suffrage; to eliminate property qualifications for officeholders, shutting off the monopoly of an elite and opening the government to the society at large; to secure fair and equal representation geographically by proportioning the lower house of the legislature to the rule of numbers; and to make a start towards local democracy by giving the people the election of certain county offices. Jefferson's constitution also embodied a number of far-reaching institutional reforms: the disestablishment of the Anglican Church and absolute religious freedom, the replacement of Virginia's bloody criminal code with one framed on humane and enlightened standards, the abolition of laws of entail and primogeniture together with other measures intended to diffuse landed property among the mass of people, and the mitigation of slavery. The Virginia Constitution of 1776 neither embodied these reforms nor envisioned them. It contained no article for future amendment or revision. Moreover, because the convention acted without delegated authority from the people, and they had not given their consent to the constitution, it lacked the essential requirements of republican legitimacy, in Jefferson's opinion.

Jefferson became a declared enemy of the Virginia Constitution. Repeatedly, over many years, he tried to replace it with a more democratic instrument, but failed. Partly because of his concern over the course of the Revolution in Virginia, he retired from Congress in September 1776, returned home, and immediately entered the General Assembly in Williamsburg. For several years, he worked to secure fundamental reforms, those already mentioned but others as well, such as a comprehensive plan of public education, viewing the whole as "a system by which ever fiber would be eradicated of ancient and feudal aristocracy, and a foundation laid for a government truly republican." [46] The reformation was at best half-successful. If, for example, the assembly finally enacted his great Bill for Religious Freedom, it flatly rejected his Bill for the More General Diffusion of Knowledge, which he came to think more important than any other for the future of freedom and self-government. He was not a flaming radical at this time, or at any time. He was a committed revolutionist, rather far to the left on the political spectrum in America; but he would not go to radical lengths to secure his objectives—his personal temperament precluded that—and he was still struggling to escape the chrysalis of the English Whig tradition, as his dilemma about the senate makes clear. What is remarkable about Jefferson, however, in contradistinction to Adams, was his capacity for political growth and adaptation. His vision was forward and he grew in democratic directions with his age and country. He came to realize that even his own ideas for Virginia's government in 1776 fell short of the principles of the Revolution. "In truth," he reflected, "the abuses of monarchy had so much filled the space of political contemplation, that we imagined everything republican which was not monarchy. We had not yet penetrated to the mother principle that 'governments are republican only in proportion as they embody the will of the people, and execute it.' "[47]

If Jefferson failed to become the republican solon of Virginia, Adams was largely successful in Massachusetts. In the fall of 1779, during an interlude between diplomatic missions abroad, he was elected by his Braintree constituents to represent them in a constitutional convention. The citizens of Massachusetts had previously rejected a constitution offered by the legislature; and part of the significance of the convention was that it would be elected by the people for the specific purpose of framing a fundamental law, which would then be referred to them for approval or disapproval. The Massachusetts constitutional convention of 1779–80 thus gave finished form to the process by which a people may establish a government with their own consent. Both Adams and Jefferson contributed to the revolutionary theory describing this process. In the convention, Adams was given the responsibility of submitting a working draft; and since few changes were made in it, either in committee or on the floor, the honor of the Massachusetts Constitution belonged to him.[48] Although it seemed designed to make as little change as possible in the customary frame of government, it was a more elaborate document than any of the constitutions Jefferson drafted for Virginia. Adams' preamble reiterated the principles of the Declaration of Independence. This was followed by a declaration of rights, derived from George Mason's seminal work engrafted on the Virginia Constitution. (Surprisingly, in view of his later position, none of Jefferson's proposed constitutions included a declaration or bill of rights.) There was more than literary significance in Adams' phrasing of certain principles generally shared with Jefferson. Thus he wrote "all men are born equally free and independent," which, as Adams knew, was not the same as saying "all men are created (or born) equal." The convention substituted Jefferson's more egalitarian accent. Adams was not responsible for Article III—the most controversial provision of the constitution—making it the duty of the legislature, and in turn of the various towns and parishes, to support religion, yet this was consistent with the aim of the document as a whole to ensure that Massachusetts remain a Christian common-wealth. Jefferson, in Virginia, was fighting a bill that would require the state to support Christian churches without pref-erence as to sect on a plan not dissimilar to that adopted in Massachusetts; and he would have found equally objectionable the religious test Adams wished to demand of officeholders. The convention eliminated the test, except for the chief magis-trate, but embarked on the new experiment in establishment of religion.

With regard to the frame of government, Adams followed the main outlines of his *Thoughts on Government*. The legislature would be in three parts, the house, the senate, and the gover-nor, as Adams conceived the British one to be. The governor would be popularly elected, which he had not proposed in 1776, and vested with large powers including an absolute nega-tive on the laws. The convention gave him only a qualified negative, or suspensive veto; but in the creation of a strong executive, overriding the antimonarchical sentiments of the Revolution, the Massachusetts Constitution was unique in its time. Increasingly, Adams viewed the executive power as the mainstay of a balanced constitution, and he thought the trim-ming of the governor's negative the only serious error of the convention. He solved the problem of the senate by propor-tioning its membership to the amount of taxes paid in the several electoral districts, that is to say, basing it on property.

The wealthier the district the more power it would have in the senate. In addition to its relevance for the Whig theory of balance, the solution conformed to the favorite axiom of James Harrington, "power always follows property," which Adams said was "as infallible a maxim in politics as that action and reaction are equal in mechanics." [49] Adams, and the convention, maintained, indeed somewhat increased, the property qualification for the franchise. Land had been widely distributed from the beginning in Massachusetts. This had not been the case in Virginia, of course; there the balance of property was against equal liberty. And so it was possible for Adams to cherish the colonial past and adhere to the Harringtonian rule consistently with his republican objectives, while for Jefferson these objectives required a break with the past and could scarcely be entertained on that rule, certainly not without reform of the laws governing landholding. Conservatism and republicanism might go together for the New Englander; they were often at odds for the Virginian. Comparatively few men were barred from the franchise in Massachusetts for want of sufficient property; nevertheless, Adams stood out against abandoning the freehold qualification. To do so would be "to confound and destroy all distinctions, and prostrate all ranks to one coarse level," he said. [50] Significantly, too, property and office were firmly joined in the Massachusetts Constitution. Representatives, senators, and the governor would be made eligible for their offices by an ascending scale of property holding. In these features Adams' frame of government was distinctly conservative, and he later thought it acquired for him "the reputation of a man of high principles and strong notions in government, scarcely compatible with republicanism." [51]

Adams was in France, on a second diplomatic mission, when the Massachusetts Constitution was ratified. Henceforth his career in the American Revolution was on the European stage where he worked in the shadow of the eminent Dr. Franklin to secure the money, arms, and friends necessary to win the war and establish American independence. With Franklin and John Jay, he was one of the negotiators of the Treaty of Peace. Jefferson, meanwhile, served as governor of Virginia during two difficult years, 1779 to 1781, which ended in the humiliation of the government and the virtual prostration of the state by British troops. He retired to Monticello under a cloud and, stung by criticism of his leadership, resolved never to return to public life. He and Adams occasionally exchanged letters about the affairs of war and the seemingly desperate cause of confederation, letters that are proof of political friendship, though not of personal intimacy. Had Jefferson kept his resolution, the friendship would have expired with the war; but he did not, in part because of the tragedy of his wife's death, and in 1784 he and Adams were back in harness together.

For Adams the American Revolution was finished. Independence had been won, new republican governments established in the states, and the confederation completed. In later years he liked to say that the Revolution was over before a drop of blood was shed or independence declared. "The revolution was in the minds and hearts of the people, and in the union of the colonies, both of which were substantially effected before hostilities commenced."[52] However admirable the patriotic sentiment, Jefferson could not agree. Adams was looking through the wrong end of the telescope. The Revolution had only fairly begun in 1776, nor had it ended in 1783. It was not past but prologue. Yet even Jefferson's anticipations fell far short of what the future would disclose. "We have it in our power to begin the world over again," *Common Sense* had declared.[53] This was inspired prophesy, the truth of which would come to Jefferson through the French Revolution rather than the American.

TWO

The French Revolution

IN 1784 CONGRESS APPOINTED THOMAS JEFFERSON MINISTER plenipotentiary on a diplomatic commission with Benjamin Franklin and John Adams to negotiate treaties of amity and commerce with the European states. Returning to public service after his wife's death, the Virginian had gone into Congress and there addressed himself to critical problems facing the new nation, among them the settlement and government of the transappalachian West and the expansion of foreign commerce. In the case of the latter, he had helped to draw up new guidelines for the European commission he would now join in Paris. The plan, which aimed at nothing less than the conversion of all Europe to the free commercial principles of the American Revolution, was a direct descendant of Adams' "plan of treaties" adopted by Congress in 1776. Calculating that its commerce, no longer monopolized by Britain, would attract the peace and friendship of Europe, the United States raised the standard of free trade and opened its doors to all nations who would recognize American independence and enter into liberal trading arrangements. The plan failed of conspicuous success except with France in 1778, where, however, the treaty of commerce was coupled with a treaty of alliance entailing political obligations at odds with the "commerce only" principle of foreign relations, of which Adams was particularly jealous. Now, in 1784, there was a new urgency behind the undertaking. Hard times had set in. The country was weak and poor. The prospects of wealth and power depended upon the expansion of foreign commerce and navigation, the dissolution of mercantilism and the liberation of trade in a widening community of nations. Britain, while not the only obstacle, stood as the most formidable one. She had lost an empire in North America but seemed determined to hold the former colonies in economic vassalage by exploiting her old mastery of the American market and excluding American carriers and productions from the West Indies, previously the most profitable branch of American trade. Congress therefore appealed to the revolutionary spirit of free trade to open new channels to American industry. This was the formidable task that brought Jefferson and Adams (and Franklin) together again, and it remained a first concern during their years on the diplomatic scene in Europe.[1]

Adams was still the senior partner in the relationship. He had, after all, except for one brief interruption, been on assignment in Europe since 1778. On the whole, it had not been a happy experience. He had not got on well with Franklin, the presiding American genius at Versailles, had quarreled with the French foreign minister, the Comte de Vergennes, and generally had made himself obnoxious to the court. Wandering off to Holland in disgust, he had planted the American standard at The Hague, and with a treaty of commerce and a loan in 1782 scored a diplomatic triumph. He was still angry at the French court for its treatment of him and for what he believed was the subserviency of Franklin and of Congress to its influence over American affairs. Franklin was an indolent old roué, a liar, intriguer, and hypocrite, a man whose reputation for philosophy and statesmanship was "one of the grossest impostures . . . practiced upon mankind since the days of Mahomet," Adams declared.[2] Vergennes aimed to keep the United States weak, divided, and dependent on France. Seeing Adams as a threat to his plans, he had, with Franklin's conniving, prevailed upon Congress in 1781 to revoke his original commission to negotiate peace and a treaty of commerce with Britain. On Adams' accounting, Congress had meanly discred-

ited the old leadership of the Adamses and Lees, the heart of
the alliance of Massachusetts and Virginia that had brought
about American independence, and fallen under the control
of a pro-French faction, which, among its other sins, treacher-
ously instructed the new peace commission to be guided by the
advice of the French ministry. Adams felt humiliated and
disgraced, not only by Congress but by his country. "It is
enough to poison the life of a man in its most secret sources,"
he confessed to an old friend.[3] After the preliminaries of the
peace were signed, Adams sent a heated protest to Congress.
The only satisfaction for the personal insult to him, he suggested, would be appointment as the first American minister to
the Court of St. James. He no longer spoke of France as "our
natural ally," Britain as "our natural enemy," her friendship
"lost forever"—his habitual language during the war—but
argued that it had never been America's interest to injure
Britain more than necessary to secure independence and that
the old friendship should now be restored as a means both of
countering French influence and of securing American trade
and prosperity.[4] This, he said, not the French alliance, was "the
cornerstone of the true American system of politics in Europe."[5] In modern diplomatic parlance, Adams was tilting
toward Britain. As it happened, however, and despite all that
Adams could do, Britain rejected the cornerstone, leaving the
Franco-American alliance intact.

   In 1784 Jefferson knew only a part of the story of Adams'
long ordeal in Europe. Virginians in Congress forewarned him
that Adams had changed. James Madison, the congressman
chiefly responsible for the revocation of Adams' 1779 commission, portrayed the New Englander as vain, pompous, envious
of Franklin, morbidly suspicious of France, and said he had
made himself ridiculous in the eyes of Congress by drawing his
own likeness for the proposed envoy to Great Britain. Jefferson was surprised. Adams' want of taste he had observed, but
vanity was "a lineament in his character" that had escaped

him.[6] (It had not escaped Adams. "The charge of vanity," he wrote in his defense, "is the last resource of little wits and mercenary quacks, the vainest men alive, against men and measures they can find no other objection to.")[7] Jefferson idolized Franklin: the man, the scientist, the statesman. They were fellow *philosophes;* their temperaments were congenial; and they thought alike about France and the French alliance. While Adams, starting with the assumption of self-interested motives on the part of France, detected subserviency in every pleasing American gesture, Franklin, and Jefferson after him, supposed these gestures cost nothing but created a spirit of mutual confidence and goodwill at the French court which served American interests. Jefferson, who would later find himself accused of subserviency to France, thought the charge against Franklin without "a shadow of a foundation." By his amiable and liberal disposition, he had, in fact, placed the French court "more under his influence, than he under theirs."[8]

The issue was partly one of diplomatic tactics and style: Franklin and Jefferson cool, supple, amiable, gracefully sliding around rough corners without losing sight of the object, Adams aggressive, candid, direct, and unyielding. But it was more substantial than that. Adams thought that nations, like individuals, were governed by avarice and ambition and were never to be trusted to motives of generosity and benevolence. Jefferson, professing "but one code of morality for man whether acting singly or collectively," thought the true interest of men and nations consistent with the dictates of morality. "I think, with others," he wrote, "that nations are to be governed according to their own interest; but I am convinced that it is their interest, in the long run, to be grateful, faithful to their engagements even in the worst of circumstances, and honorable and generous always."[9] The moral question of gratitude to France for her assistance in the American Revolution was thus assimilated to a philosophy of higher self-interest; and

since France alone gave the United States a place to stand from
which to exert influence in Europe, he was a staunch advocate
of the French alliance. Adams, on the other hand, while he
usually recognized the expediency of the alliance, remained
uncomfortable with it and resented any idea of moral obligation to France.

The composition of the Paris commission seemed a perfect
recipe for discord, yet Adams was soon writing of "the wonderful harmony, good humor, and unanimity" of the three men.
Perhaps this was owing to Jefferson's presence, for both Adams
and Franklin were happy with him. Some of the former's
friends had tried to plant suspicions of the Virginian in his
mind, but without success. "He is an old friend," Adams said,
"with whom I have often had occasion to labor at many a knotty
problem, and in whose abilities and steadiness I always found
great cause to confide."[10] He discovered no reason to change
his opinion or to doubt Jefferson's partialities for any country
but his own. After many months Jefferson reached a judicious
assessment of Adams. Madison, to whom he wrote, was partly
right. "He is vain, irritable, and a bad calculator of the force
and probable effect of the motives which govern men. This,"
however, "is all the ill which can possibly be said of him. He is as
disinterested as the being which made him; he is profound in
his views, and accurate in his judgments except where knowledge of the world is necessary to form a judgment. He is so
amiable, that I pronounce you will love him if ever you become
acquainted with him."[11] Outside the line of official business,
Jefferson saw little of Franklin, ailing and almost a recluse at
Passy, but he became an intimate of the Adams family installed
in an airy mansion at Auteuil. Abigail and the children, including young John Quincy, were charmed by the tall Virginian's
gracious manners and conversation. "He is one of the choice
ones of the earth," Abigail said.[12] The circle of affection, which
included Jefferson's daughter Martha, strengthened the bond
between the two men. They would be separated in the spring

of 1785 when Congress at last appointed Adams minister to Great Britain and at the same time named Jefferson as Franklin's successor at Versailles. The Adamses' departure left Jefferson "in the dumps." From London Abigail wrote of how loath she had been "to leave behind me the only person with whom my companion could associate with perfect freedom and unreserve." [13] But the two envoys, the only Americans of rank in Europe, were in constant communication as they labored for their country's cause.

Although the European-wide commission continued for another year, it was obviously a failure, with only a Prussian treaty to its credit, and the American ministers focused their commercial diplomacy on Britain and France. They were in substantial agreement on the objectives: first, to relieve the agonies of American commerce by obtaining favors abroad; second, to forward the new ideal of "perfect liberty" of trade as in the ultimate interest of all nations; third, to strengthen the struggling confederation at home by means of treaties which would bring the foreign commerce of the states under the jurisdiction of Congress; and fourth, to steer clear of political entanglements with Europe. Variations of outlook appeared in the pursuit of these objectives, of course. Jefferson, installed in the liberal circle of Turgot's disciples and the physiocrats in Paris, was the more philosophical and persevering, Adams the more immediately practical and easily discouraged by unpleasant realities. Jefferson decided that France held the key to America's commercial problem and, eventually, to the wider free-trade system. If France would improve upon the existing treaty, abolish antiquated restrictions, open her ports freely to American ships and raw materials, and pay for them in manufactures, wines, tropical produce, and so on, the British monopoly would be broken and other nations must follow the course of liberation. While admiring his friend's resourceful efforts at Versailles, Adams smiled at these grand hopes and worried over the political consequences of a Franco-American

commercial axis. In the final analysis, however, Adams had no
choice but to support Jefferson's strategy. He found nothing
but contempt for the United States in Britain and no disposition whatever to negotiate a commercial treaty when by her
restrictive policy Britain commanded the American market
and three-fourths of the navigation between the two countries.
After Massachusetts retaliated with a navigation act in 1785,
Adams applauded the move and hoped the other states would
follow. Britain, with preternatural determination to reverse
the outcome of the war, had commenced commercial hostilities
and the United States had to defend itself. "We must not, my
friend," he wrote his philosophical colleague in Paris, "be the
bubbles of our own liberal sentiments. If we cannot obtain
reciprocal liberality, we must adopt reciprocal prohibitions,
exactions, monopolies, and imposts." [14] Jefferson agreed, and
both recognized that the states must become "one nation"
commercially through a stronger federal union before economic retaliation could succeed. As to France, Adams reluc-
tantly went along with Jefferson's policy of multiplying connec-
tions "both commercial and political." [15]

In March 1786 Jefferson joined Adams in London on several
items of official business and came away with all his prejudices
against the "rich, proud, hectoring, swearing, squibbing, car-
nivorous" English nation confirmed.[16] Carried to court by his
friend, who had been cordially received a year before, Jefferson was snubbed and humiliated by George III. Nor did he
find much friendliness anywhere. "That nation hates us," he
concluded, "their ministers hate us, and their king more than
all other men." [17] Pleasure mixed with business as Jefferson,
Adams in tow, made a tour of the celebrated English gardens,
the country style of which he infinitely preferred to the formal
classical taste of the French. With the eyes of a connoisseur,
who believed that America should have "the noblest gardens"
and who meant to set an example at Monticello, Jefferson
dutifully noted every slope of a lawn, drop of a cascade, size of

a lake or pond, style of an arch, effect of a statue or temple, and cost of a grotto. Adams did not share his enthusiasm. Such luxury and magnificence could not be reconciled with virtuous republicanism. "It will be long, I hope, before ridings, parks, pleasure grounds, gardens, and ornamental farms grow so much in fashion in America," he jotted in his diary.[18] Jefferson understood the point, but he did not allow his chaste republicanism to drown his aesthetic sensibilities.

In their response to the Old World—"the vaunted scene of Europe," Jefferson called it—the Virginian and the New Englander were almost stereotypically American. Indeed, they helped to create the stereotype. Yet their responses were qualitatively different, as their encounter with the English gardens suggests. Neither found any good in European governments. The opulence and tyranny of kings and nobles, the oppression and misery of the mass of people presented no other picture, said Jefferson, "than that of God almighty and his angels trampling under foot the hosts of the damned," and, of course, made any idea of a revolution on the American plan virtually inconceivable. "My God!" he exclaimed to a friend at home. "How little do my countrymen know what precious blessings they are in possession of, and which no other people on earth enjoy. I confess I had no idea of it myself."[19] The revelation suggests how far Jefferson's odyssey abroad led him into intellectual possession of that "American dream" born in Europe but destined to mature in America, partly under his auspices.

Adams made the same discovery, but it did not have the same impact on him. He was more accepting of the old regime in Europe, as if it were decreed by fate or history. (He thought it important to assure Lafayette that he was "no king-killer, king-hater, or king-despiser.")[20] An ingrained religious prejudice left him skeptical of republicanism in any country where Roman Catholicism held sway or, conversely, where atheism was so much in fashion as in France. European morals were, if anything, worse than European politics. On his initiation into

Parisian society during the Revolution, Adams was shocked by
the looseness of conversation and the spirit of female intrigue.
Marital infidelity corrupted everything, including government. The manners of women were the best barometer of the
state of morals in a nation, he reasoned, for the foundations of
morality were laid in the family if they were laid anywhere.
Jefferson was no puritan, but he too warned Americans against
European debauchery and vice.[21] The saving grace of Europe,
of France in particular, for him was the civility of manners and
the artistic splendor he found everywhere. "Here," he wrote,
"it seems that a man might pass a life without encountering a
single rudeness. . . . Were I to proceed to tell you how much I
enjoy their architecture, sculpture, painting, music, I should
want words."[22] Adams conceded the elegance and the splendor. "But what is this to me?" asked this self-styled "stern and
haughty republican." "I receive but little pleasure in beholding
all these things, because I cannot but consider them as baga-
telles, introduced by time and luxury in exchange for the . . .
hardy manly virtues of the human heart."[23] Jefferson was not
assailed in his republican convictions by Europe's civilizing
arts. They were, rather, worthy of the emulation of the new
nation. Thus he designed a noble capitol for Virginia based on
a classical model, the Masion Carrée at Nîmes, thereby inau-
gurating the Roman style in the public architecture of the
United States. "You see," he wrote in this connection, "I am
an enthusiast on the subject of the arts. But it is an enthusiasm
of which I am not ashamed, as its object is to improve the taste
of my countrymen, to increase their reputation, and to recon-
cile to them the respect of the world and procure them its
praise."[24] Adams thought Jefferson was putting the cart before
the horse. "It is not indeed the fine arts which our country
requires," he told Abigail. It was his duty as an American to
study government to the exclusion of all other arts and sciences. "I must study politics and war, that my sons may have

the liberty to study mathematics and philosophy . . . in order to
give their sons a right to study painting, poetry, music, architecture, statuary, tapestry, and porcelain." [25] This would
prove to be good prophesy for successive generations of the
Adams family; but Jefferson's timetable and scale of values
were different.

   With his scale of values, and with a set of provincial prejudices his character could not conceal, Adams never felt at home
in Europe, while for Jefferson the five years he spent there
were among the happiest of his life. Already, before he left
America, he was an infant *philosophe*, a disciple of the Enlightenment, that "mixture of classicism, impiety, and science," [26] headquartered in Paris, and he soon found himself
placed in the best circles and salons. The Marquis de Chastel-
lux, who had earlier encountered him at Monticello, introduced him in flattering colors to the philosophical public in his
Travels. And with the publication of his *Notes on the State of
Virginia*, Jefferson attained a scientific and literary reputation
second only to Franklin among Americans. He was not only an
American but a cosmopolitan, one who cared as much for the
commerce of ideas as the commerce of tobacco, and one to
whom liberal Frenchmen naturally turned for instruction
when they set out to reform their own government. Adams,
although a man of the Enlightenment (more accurately of the
earlier mid-century Enlightenment) in his political opinions,
was neither of the mind nor the party of *philosophes*. Their
naturalistic creed, he thought "neither more nor less than the
creed of Epicurus set to the music of Lucretius," and he read
their books chiefly for the pleasure of denunciation. [27] He had
thus found himself an outsider in Paris for reasons that struck
deeper than rigidity of personality and deficiency in the *je ne
sais quoi* of fashionable society. [28] Yet, paradoxical though it
may seem, it was Adams, the Yankee provincial, who became
the captive of European political fears and transferred them to

America, while Jefferson, the cosmopolitan philosopher, matured a self-conscious American idealism from his perspective
in Europe.

   Central to this development was the French Revolution, but
before that event Adams wrote a book which froze his politics
into a system at odds with democratic aspirations in both
Europe and America. His *Defence of the American Constitutions,*
1787, was a three-volume demonstration of the thesis that the
"unum necessarium" of republican liberty and order is the tripartite division of the legislative power, each of the branches
embodying a distinctive social and political principle—the one,
the few, and the many; monarchy, aristocracy, and democracy
—and by a kind of Newtonian mechanics maintaining the
equilibrium of the whole.[29] Adams commenced the work, a
disordered pastiche of the writings on European governments
from ancient to modern interspersed with his own comments,
in the fall of 1786. What set him off was the news of popular
insurgency against the government in Massachusetts. But in
Adams' mind, Shays' Rebellion (as it was soon named) was only
the culmination of a course of degeneracy he had been observing in the United States for several years. Virtue had declined,
the spirit of faction had appeared; class conflict reared its head,
elections grew corrupt, and the people ran wild with false
notions of liberty and equality. How else, except on some such
hypothesis, was Adams to account for his country's ingratitude
to himself? America was going the way of Europe and would
have to heed the uniform lessons of European experience. The
dangers evoked by Shays' Rebellion seemed to call for an
urgent program of instruction, which Adams sought to provide. He was also motivated by gloomy forebodings over the
course of events in Europe. The *Defence* had a European
address as well as an American one. His Dutch friends were
locked in struggle with prince and oligarchs. The Assembly of
Notables was only four months away in Paris. "The fountains
of the great deep were broken up in France," Adams later

recalled, "and the proud wave of democracy was spreading and swelling and rolling, not only through that kingdom, but into England, Holland, Geneva, and Switzerland, and, indeed, threatening an inundation over all Europe." While in spirit on the side of the reformers, Adams was skeptical of their success and of one thing was absolutely sure: "that if they aimed at any constitution more popular than the English, they would ruin themselves, after setting Europe on fire and shedding oceans of blood."[30]

Despite the work's title, it was a defense of the American constitutions in only the most cryptic and roundabout fashion. The constitutions of two-thirds of the states were indefensible, Adams conceded to Jefferson. They were no better than those of the petty Italian republics of the late middle ages, to which Adams devoted his second volume, and they were destined to end the same way.[31] The work was, in reality, a defense of the true theory of republican constitutions against an attack mounted by the late great *philosophe*, Turgot. Turgot had criticized the Americans for copying European (mainly British) forms and practices and thus failing to fix their governments on the principles of nature and reason. Instead of collecting all authority in one center as the logic of equality and popular sovereignty dictated, the new constitutions endeavored to create an equilibrium of power among different orders of men and principles of government in pale imitation of the English king, lords, and commons. The criticism tallied with Thomas Paine's democratic opinions in 1776. Adams' reply, a long one, was that the history of governments proved the tripartite balance of power to be, in fact, the fundamental principle of reason and nature, as infallible as the demonstrations of Euclid. It was realized most perfectly in the English constitution, which Adams pronounced "the only scientific government" in the world. Government ought to be founded on the laws of human nature rather than on philosophical visions of perfectibility. History is the vast storehouse of facts about human nature. Adams ransacked history. And what it showed was, first, that all men are creatures of passion, for fame or power or wealth; second, that they are always divided into the few and the many, the rich and the poor, the aristocrats and the commoners; and third, that these two great orders of society are constantly threatening to destroy each other. Having discovered this theory of behavior in history, Adams then read all history in terms of the theory. Because the nature of man does not change, neither does the nature of government. In the *Defence* the same dreary round of ambition and conflict, sedition and corruption, war and revolution is reported over and over again, relieved occasionally, however, in those states that find for a time the *deus ex machina*, the tripartite balance. This involves, above all, erecting a third power, a monarchical executive, to serve as an umpire or a balance wheel between the democracy and the aristocracy. It involves, in addition, the constitution of these two orders into separate and distinct representative assemblies. Neither alone nor in superiority can secure the liberties of the republic. The people are as despotic as kings and nobles: Adams was the first modern political theorist to speak of "the tyranny of the majority." The aristocracy of birth, wealth, and talents, although it has limitless capacity for harm, is the best part of the state if it is properly managed. Allow it to mix with the people and it will subvert them, allow it any share of the executive power and it will bring down the constitution; but "ostracize" the aristocracy to one assembly and its vices may be curbed to the advantage of its virtues. The invidious competition between the two great classes of society is rendered useful when they are made to control each other and a monarchical executive is installed as the presiding genius over the whole. Such was the political science of John Adams.

Jefferson read Adams' first volume just as the Assembly of Notables convened in Paris. Writing to the author, he praised "its learning and good sense," thought it would do "great good" in America, and said he would arrange for a French translation.[32] It would be wrong to conclude from these generous comments that Jefferson was therefore in fundamental accord with the doctrines of the *Defence*. He did not care to dispute philosophical differences with friends. Almost instinctively, he accommodated himself to the feelings of others without compromising his own opinions. He liked Franklin's rule, "Never contradict anybody," and tended to express personal approval or disapproval by varying degrees of assent. He never attempted to throw his own thought into a system, in part because he distrusted all theoretical systems. As a result, while Adams' political science is readily identified, Jefferson's remains formless and elusive. Undoubtedly, Jefferson felt greater sympathy for Adams' system in 1787 than he would several years later, after its tendencies were more fully disclosed by the French Revolution and political developments in the United States. But even in 1787, though he agreed with the general idea of constitutional balance, Jefferson was seriously at issue with his friend on many points.

Jefferson did not share Adams' fears of popular tumult and insurrection. Shays' Rebellion had presented to him the not unpleasing picture of American liberty flexing its muscles. The "spirit of resistance to government" was always valuable, and infinitely perferable to European despotism. "I like a little rebellion now and then," he told the Adamses. "It is like a storm in the atmosphere." [33] Adams' appeal to history for the laws of nature, his vision of the political past as a timeless void, fixed and unchanging in its basic rhythms, his use of history to puncture the hopes of philosophers for the improvability and progress of mankind—all this ran against Jefferson's mental grain. Adams' portrayal of the English constitution must have appeared to him as a caricature of the real thing, while his advocacy of a monarchical executive flew in the face of America's revolutionary experience. Making some exception for Massachusetts, every American constitution—those constitutions Adams was purportedly defending—stripped the executive office of monarchical features. But the greatest puzzle of all was the wide disparity between Adams' theory of government by orders, allegedly founded in the nature of things, and the realities of American society. As Adams himself sometimes conceded, there was but one order in America: all men were commoners. Yet he insisted on applying the Old World norms of the one, the few, and the many. These abstractions had troubled Jefferson too, as in his effort to find a quasi-aristocratic basis for the senate in Virginia; but, with other American Whigs, he had worked his way out of the difficulty. Recognizing that the people were all one, undifferentiated in their rights and sovereignty, he had replaced the traditional theory of balanced government with the newer functional theory of separation of powers, in which legislative, executive, and judicial powers, all derivative of the people, checked and balanced each other. As for the senate, it simply doubled the representation, and protection, of the people. This became the constitutional safeguard against the inherent tendency of power to corrupt and of every government to degenerate into despotism.[34] Adams was still enthralled by the traditional theory. When confronted with American egalitarianism, he replied that it was a delusion, that real distinctions of rank persisted, that the semblance of three orders remained even if the things themselves did not, though in time the orders would mature and a hereditary chief magistracy and an aristocratic senate would probably become necessary to secure the republic against popular violence and corruption. America had discovered no new principles of society and government. There could be no new principles. "Our experience . . . corresponds with that of all ages and nations," Adams wrote. And if only the names were changed, the future of Massachusetts or New York or the states collectively could be read in the history of Florence or Siena or Pistoia.[35]

Many of Adams' friends would later look back to the *Defence of the American Constitutions* as the turning point in his politics, away from republican principles to monarchical and aristocratic principles; and he himself came to believe that this book, more belied than any since the Bible, he said, utterly destroyed his reputation. In 1787–88, however, the book was well received (there were three editions within the year) in the United States. Its appearance coincided with the new federal Constitution. Adams liked to think that it exerted an influence on the Constitution. This was not the case, but its high political tone suited the Constitution's advocates, the Federalists.

The two American envoys held their own little debate on the Constitution. Jefferson confessed, on first reading it, that it staggered all his dispositions. The old system of the Articles of Confederation was too weak, but this new plan seemed too strong. The demigods at Philadelphia, he feared, had over-reacted to the insurrection in Massachusetts: "they are setting up a kite to keep the hen yard in order."[36] Writing to Adams, he sharply criticized the Constitution for allowing perpetual reeligibility of the president. A president reeligible every fourth year might easily become a president for life, a king, albeit an elective one, like the king of Poland, and like him the center of foreign intrigue, bribery, and force.[37] Adams' principal objection ran to the opposite: the president was too weak and dependent. He rejoiced that the executive had been made part of the legislature, with at least a suspensive veto, but condemned the intrusion of the senate in matters of treaties and appointments to office. This would lessen the public responsibility of the president while at the same time exciting the insatiable ambitions of the senate. "You are afraid of the one—I, of the few," he told Jefferson. "You are apprehensive of Monarchy, I, of Aristocracy." As to the protest that a president once chosen would serve for life, so much the better. "You are apprehensive of foreign interference, intrigue, influence. So am I. But, as often as elections happen, the danger of foreign influence recurs. The less frequently they happen the less danger."[38] The more Jefferson studied the Constitution, the more he approved of it. He yielded his objection to presidential reeligibility, after learning that it aroused no fears in the United States, and concentrated instead on the attainable improvement, the addition of a bill of rights.[39] Adams, meanwhile, expressing no concern for this addition, began to worry about the uncertain sovereignty of government under the Constitution. Unless it was "wholly national," rather than a new experiment in divided sovereignty—"a fresh essay at imperium in imperio"—the Constitution would be a rope of sand.[40] Jefferson, on the other hand, thought the ingenious mixing of two governments, state and national, each supreme in its sphere, the Constitution's best feature. In the principle of federalism he found another, and thoroughly practical, safeguard of liberty, one which never entered into Adams' system of political balance.

After eight years in Europe, Adams was preparing to return home. He was tired, of course, useless and virtually friendless in England, and neither his own honor nor that of Congress would permit him to remain minister to a court that treated the United States with haughty contempt. What the future held for him he did not know. Perhaps he would retire to his fireside and ruminate on the follies of mankind. At any rate, he would leave Europe with but two regrets: the loss of the opportunity afforded by a plentitude of books for researching questions in the science of government, and the interruption of his correspondence with Jefferson, which he called one of the most agreeable events of his life. Jefferson, upon whom the entire burden of American affairs in Europe would now rest, said he felt "bewidowed." He had leaned on Adams' judgment and was especially anxious about "the department of money," long under Adams' management. The Dutch bankers, whose loans had kept the confederation afloat, sent up distress signals for American credit just as the country moved toward a government intended to secure it. Adams had seen enough of "the unmeasurable avarice of Amsterdam," but he met there with Jefferson early in the new year, and together they negotiated a loan to provide for American needs during the transition to the new government. In February 1788, Adams sailed for home.

For Jefferson, as he wrote to Abigail, it was the end of an epoch. It was the end of one epoch and the beginning of another in Europe too. The continent was turbulent from the Black Sea to the North. The Russians and the Turks were at war. In Holland, a bourgeois democratic revolution had been defeated and its leaders, who had been instructed in the American Revolution by John Adams, were cruelly suppressed or driven into exile by the Stadtholder, William V, Prince of Orange, in league with the old oligarchs and with the intervention of Britain and Prussia. Adams and Jefferson agonized for the Dutch Patriots, but felt that they had been betrayed by their own excesses as well as by their Bourbon ally. The fact that France, pledged to the Patriots, had not lifted a finger in their support offered a melancholy lesson for the United States. "In fact," Jefferson wrote to his friend, "what a crowd of lessons do the present miseries of Holland teach us. Never to have an hereditary officer of any sort; never to let a citizen ally himself with kings; never to call in foreign nations to settle domestic differences; never to suppose that any nation will expose itself to war for us etc." [41] War was averted over the Dutch question, but France sank in the scales of power while Britain rose and might think the time propitious for regaining her lost American colonies. "Oh fortunate Americans, if you did but know your own felicity!" Adams wrote home. [42] But they did not, and if they did would be unable to keep it. Jefferson's "lessons" would be as little heeded in America as elsewhere. "The loss of paradise, by eating a forbidden apple, has been many thousand years a lesson to mankind; but not much regarded." Resolutions never to have an hereditary officer would be kept until the Society of Cincinnati or some other blood-proud faction chose to violate them; resolutions never to allow a citizen to ally himself with kings only until some duke or dauphin demanded an American daughter in marriage; resolutions never to invite the intervention of foreign nations only until a serious domestic crisis arose. "I have long been settled in my own opinion," he told Jefferson, "that neither philosophy, nor religion, nor morality, nor wisdom, nor interest, will ever govern nations or parties, against their vanity, their pride, their resentment or revenge, or their avarice or ambition. Nothing but force and power and strength can restrain them."[43] These reflections, which drew no response from Paris, were perfectly consonant with the doctrines of Adams' book and also with his gloomy forebodings for the revolution in France that had already seized upon Jefferson's sanguine heart.

Jefferson was a partisan of the French Revolution from the start. In the liberal circles of Paris, where American scripture was quoted like the Bible in Rome, he stood as the oracle of the revolutionary nation that inspired France. He could not have remained passive or silent even if he had wanted to. The revolution became, of course, much more than he or anyone envisioned in its early stages. For two and one-half years, while he remained minister to France, and then after he returned to the United States, Jefferson had repeatedly to adjust his thinking to a course of events always leaping ahead of him. He kept expecting the movement to come to rest, the revolution to stabilize itself at some reasonable point along the line of advance. When it did not but rolled dizzily onward with an egalitarian energy he had not suspected, Jefferson hurried to catch up and offer counsels of conciliation at the next favorable turn. Like some of his liberal friends, he hoped for a final settlement more on the terms of the English constitution than the American. A nation could not go from despotism to liberty all at once. A limited constitutional monarchy, with a regular parliament and guarantees of certain individual liberties, would be a great gain for the nation, and Jefferson doubted France was ready for more. In this he was not far from Adams' opinion. But Jefferson, for all his apparent moderation, never hesitated to follow, then to cheer, the more radical course once it was chosen. Adams' response to the French Revolution was to "rejoice with trembling," as he said.[44] And he turned increasingly against it as it veered from the conservative direction he thought it should follow. Jefferson went with the revolution, and as it grew more and more radical, so did Jefferson.

In the preliminary stage opened by the Assembly of Notables in 1787, Jefferson supported the aristocratic resurgence against royal absolutism in the belief it would yield needed reforms. He was especially pleased by the plan to introduce provincial assemblies, a reform advocated by Turgot's disciples, which would circumscribe the power of the crown and give the people a voice. Moreover, the game had been so played in the assembly that the concession was obtained without paying the king's price: consent to new taxes that would fall most heavily on the nobility. The evils of monarchical power loomed so large in Jefferson's mind that he seemed to overlook the aristocratic animus of the entire movement. The *noblesse*, the *parlements*, and other aristocratic bodies had no intention of surrendering their privileged status, of agreeing to equal taxes, or, in fact, of allowing the provincial assemblies to be representative of the people. Had Adams been right when he told Jefferson, "You are afraid of the one—I, of the few"? So it sometimes appeared. Basically, however, the observation falsifies the political thought of both men. Adams feared aristocracy, but he also deemed aristocracy essential to the preservation of liberty; indeed he could assert that so far as liberty had been preserved in European states, it was the work of nobles operating between kings and peoples. Neither the one nor the few, Jefferson believed, could exist without the other. According to Montesquieu, nobility entered into the essence of monarchy, which had as its fundamental axiom, "No monar-

chy, no nobility; no nobility, no monarch." [45] If the two orders
were often opposed, they were also mutually dependent; and
in the end they would succor each other rather than succor the
people, as European experience made plain during the age of
democratic revolution. But where as in France there was no
people in any meaningful political sense, Jefferson supposed
that the nobility offered the only logical starting point for
reformation, and that it must begin with the monarchy. He
may have been right in this. The aristocratic revolt, narrowly
conceived though it was, forced an appeal to the nation.

"The gay and thoughtless Paris has now become a furnace of
politics," Jefferson reported in the spring of 1788. "All the
world is run politically mad. Men, women, children talk nothing else." [46] As the controversy widened, he saw with increasing
clarity that neither of the centuries' old contenders, king or
nobility, was capable of acting for the good of the people. "The
king and the *parlement* [of Paris] are quarreling for the oyster.
The shell will be left as heretofore to the people." [47] Unfortunately, the people were not yet ripe for the blessings of liberty
and self-government. They could not act for what they did not
know. Jefferson doubted they would accept a habeas corpus
law if it were handed to them. "The danger is that the people,"
he said, "deceived by a false cry of liberty may be led to take side
with one party, and thus give the other a pretext for crushing them still more." [48] Something like this had happened in
Holland, Jefferson thought, and the fiasco of the democratic
revolution there colored his counsels to the French. The
monarchists and aristocrats had contested for monopoly, but
when the Patriots frightened the latter with the loss of the
common prey, they combined with the Stadtholder and left the
people victims as before. Jefferson felt events would take a
happier turn in France, however. [49]

His confidence centered on the historic convening of the
Estates General. The Third Estate, the heretofore powerless
people, was invited into the revolution; but whether it would

have effective voice depended on the resolution of two issues with the privileged orders. Jefferson's friends in the "patriot party," including the Duc de La Rochefoucauld, the Marquis de Condorcet, Pierre Samuel Dupont, and, of course, the Marquis de Lafayette, demanded that the Third Estate have as many deputies as the nobles and clergy combined, then called for voting by head rather than order in the assembly. The first demand prevailed over angry aristocratic opposition, while the second was left to the decision of the Estates General itself. The king was now virtually out of the contest, Jefferson reported to Adams at home in Braintree in December.[50] A liberal constitutional reformation was within the grasp of the patriot leaders, provided they did not overreach themselves, shocking the conciliatory dispositions of the ministry and provoking the vengeance of the privileged orders. Jefferson grew bolder, siding unequivocally with the Third Estate, yet maintained his position as a prudent counselor of moderation.

When the Estates General convened in May 1789, a crisis at once occurred on the demand of the Third that the three orders coalesce in a single national assembly. Now for the first time, Jefferson said, the revolution "begins to wear a fearful appearance." As the stalemate entered the fifth week, he proposed to his friends a "charter of rights" to be brought forth by the king and signed by every deputy of the three orders. The charter would grant the right of the Estates General to convene regularly, to raise and appropriate money, and to legislate with the king's consent; it would provide for the abolition of fiscal privileges, and by a declaration of rights guarantee fundamental civil liberties.[51] In its goals the plan marked still another advance in Jefferson's conception of the revolution, one still grounded, however, in an accommodation of king, nobles, and commoners, more in the spirit of the English Revolution of 1688 than the American of 1776. Thirty years later, when he wrote his personal account of the coming of the French Revolution, Jefferson felt that events had vindicated his judgment

and proved the "lamentable error" of those nameless Frenchmen responsible for rejecting the compromise. "For after
thirty years of war, foreign and domestic, the loss of millions of
lives, the prostration of private happiness, and the foreign
subjugation of their own country for a time, they have obtained
no more, nor even that securely."[52] Adams would surely have
agreed. But Jefferson was right only if an amiable compromise
such as he had advocated was politically feasible in 1789. And it
was not. The revolution rapidly passed the stage of constitutional reformation arranged from above and became a vast
social upheaval against order and privilege.

The immediate crisis was resolved by the submission of the
clergy and nobility and the formation of a single national
assembly. Jefferson still hoped for a peaceful revolution, with
the establishment of a stable constitution, relying on moderate
elements in the assembly backed by the king. If the king had
sided openly with the revolution, the opportunity might have
been realized. But Louis XVI, while honest and good, was
weak, wholly dominated by the queen and the "Turkish despots" of the court; and as Jefferson put it succinctly, "the
expediency of a hereditary aristocracy is too difficult a question
for him."[53] The king rallied to the *noblesse*, resorted to force,
provoked the violence of the populace, and dug the grave of
the old regime. Jefferson was witness to the momentous events
of July—the storming of the Bastille, the arming of the populace, the mobs and savage murders of obnoxious aristocrats—
and said that he so clearly saw the legitimacy of these things
that he was untroubled by them.[54] By August he had embraced
not only the radical goals of the French Revolution but the
idea, at first inculcated by Americanists like Lafayette and
philosophes like Condorcet, that it belonged to the same political
universe as the American Revolution. The nation, Jefferson
wrote, "has made a total resumption of rights, which they had
certainly never before ventured even to think of. The National

Assembly have now as clean a canvas to work on here as we had in America." [55]

After the so-called abolition of feudalism and adoption of the Declaration of the Rights of Man and Citizen, the National Assembly turned to the formation of a constitution; and here Adams returned to the scene as an important, if absent, figure in the debate. Jefferson, it may be recalled, had promised to arrange for the publication of the *Defence of the American Constitutions* in France. Translation was at once begun, yet to Adams' chagrin nothing appeared until 1792 and that only an abridgment of his work. This was more than accidental. Jefferson soon learned, in 1787, that liberal philosophers and men-of-letters in Paris disapproved of the book. They were, for the most part, the disciples of Turgot, whom Adams attacked, and the friends of Jefferson—the same men who formed the nucleus of the Patriot party. [56] The *Defence*, in their opinion, outdid Montesquieu's *Esprit des lois*, whose political authority they were trying to dispel, in idolatry of the English constitution and advocacy of aristocratic institutions. There is no evidence that Jefferson conspired with his friends to prevent publication of the *Defence*, but it seems likely that under their prodding he became a conscious critic of Adams' book, as he did also of Montesquieu's, and lost interest in its publication. Condorcet replied to the *Defence* in his *Letters of a Gentleman of New Haven . . . to a Citizen of Virginia* (perhaps a disguise for Jefferson) in 1788. The following year he and Dupont brought out a French translation, with elaborate notes and commentary, of the American John Stevens' *Observations on Government*, a vigorous attack on the *Defence* as a mockery of the popular governments of the United States. [57] Many of Jefferson's friends in Paris, wishing a government formed as closely as possible on the American model, were embarrassed by Adams' book. They looked to Jefferson for support, and in the controversy surrounding the new French constitution, he came to

see the retrograde tendencies of Adams' politics for a reform-
ing Europe as well as for America.

The controversy centered on two main questions. Should
the king (and no party proposed to abolish the monarchy) have
an absolute or suspensive veto of legislation? And should the
legislature be in one or two houses? The American minister,
setting aside the proprieties, presided over a dinner meeting at
his house during which some of the Patriot leaders, themselves
divided, discussed these issues at length. The decision favored
a suspensive veto and a single assembly chosen by the people.
"This concordate decided the fate of the constitution," Jefferson later wrote. "The Patriots all rallied to the principles thus
settled, carried every question agreeably to them, and reduced
the aristocracy to impotence."[58] Meanwhile, from the United
States, Adams advocated directly the opposite course: an absolute negative in the king and a bicameral legislature, recon-
stituting the two great classes in separate houses, nobles and
commons, with the clergy divided between them.[59] In the
National Assembly the *Defence* was cited as authority for the
latter position especially. In principle, Jefferson also favored
two houses, but on the new American theory of checks and
balances within a uniformly republican legislature, not on the
theory of estates or orders. He recognized, however, that any
upper house in France would become the asylum of aristocracy
and raise havoc with the revolution. The safety of a divided
legislature was perfectly compatible with democracy in America, whereas it would defeat democracy in France. Theory and
practice were at variance, a variance Adams' system could not
admit.

Jefferson left France in the fall for what he supposed was a
brief leave of absence at home. The revolution had made great
strides and dragged him with it. A long and rocky road still lay
ahead. Jefferson was prepared for setbacks. As he later philos-
ophized to Lafayette, "we are not . . . to be translated from
despotism to liberty in a featherbed."[60] But he returned home

full of optimism. He felt he had witnessed, as twenty years before in America, the commencement of a new era in Europe. "I have so much confidence in the good sense of man, and his qualifications for self-government," he declared, "that I am never afraid of the issue where reason is left free to exert her force; and I will agree to be stoned as a false prophet if all does not end well in this country. Nor will it end with this country. Here is but the first chapter in the history of European liberty."[61] He was consumed by this cause. It was America's, of course, but five years before, when he went abroad, he had had little idea of its becoming Europe's. Experience had changed him in seemingly contradictory ways. Seeing his own country from the perspective of Europe, he had become more self-consciously American, an "apostle of Americanism" in the judgment of one biographer. But the French Revolution had also furthered his education in democracy, which he would mature into a political ideology, and extended his vision of America's responsibility for advancing the freedom of mankind. America became a mirror for Europe. His friend Adams, on the other hand, had made Europe into a mirror of his anxieties for America. The two worlds became blurred in his mind. European political doctrine was applied to America; American doctrine was applied to Europe; and neither offered much hope for liberty, equality, and fraternity.

Early in 1790 the two Americans were reunited in New York, the temporary capital of the new government. Adams had been elected vice-president and Jefferson had become secretary of state at President Washington's invitation. The New Englander was unhappy in his new position. The salary was beneath the station of the "heir apparent," and the circumstances of his election, with just over half the electoral votes given to Washington, had been insulting. He had then made himself an object of ridicule by championing a high-sounding title for the president and official forms and ceremonies reminiscent of British royalty. Convinced that the new govern-

ment was, or ought to be, a "monarchical republic," he thought
the president should have a title commensurate with the office.
Nothing less than "His Majesty," "His Most Benign Highness,"
or, as a Senate committee recommended, "His Highness, President of the United States, and Protector of the Liberties of the
Same" would do. His intent was not to make the president a
king, but to lend honor and dignity to the government, draw
forth the best talents, command the respect of foreign courts,
and awe the wayward populace. "Neither dignity nor authority
can be supported in human minds . . . ," he told Washington,
"without splendor and majesty in some degree proportioned
to them."[62] Adams had learned this lesson in Europe. The
titles, ceremonies, and shows of crowned heads, "the coup de
theâtre" of politics, might be condemned by philosophy, but
they were the attractive force of every government, as of every
religion, and all the more necessary in America because of the
absence of hereditary rank and distinction.[63] Indeed, an attack
on titles and ceremonies was an attack on government itself.
Jefferson, who prayed for the disappearance of all titles but
"Mister," heard of Adams' campaign in Paris. It reminded him
of Franklin's characterization of the New Englander: "always
an honest man, often a wise one, but sometimes, and in some
things, absolutely out of his senses."[64] Mercifully, Congress
settled on the simple title, "The President of the United
States." The portly vice-president was not so fortunate: he
became "His Rotundity."

Adams' honest, if foolish, campaign for titles contributed to
the growing opinion that he had changed his politics while
abroad. Confronted with this charge by his old friend Benjamin Rush, he indignantly denied it. Yet in letters to Rush and
other correspondents he did not disguise his belief that
hereditary monarchy and aristocracy would eventually prove
as necessary to the American republic as they had to every
other. These were, he told Rush, "the only institutions that can
possibly preserve the laws and liberties of the people, and I am

clear that Americans must resort to them as an asylum against discord, seditions, and civil war, and that at no very distant period of time. . . . I think it therefore impolitic to cherish prejudices against institutions which must be kept in view as the hope of our posterity. I am," he continued, "by no means for attempting any such thing at present. Our country is not yet ripe for it in many respects, and it is not necessary, but our ship must ultimately land on that shore or be cast away."[65] This is as fair a statement of Adams' opinion as one is apt to find. He spoke of change in the future tense, and more with regret than rejoicing, yet his present tense was so condemnatory that no one could be blamed for questioning his commitment to the democratic republic. In 1790, as the congressional elections came on, Adams voiced old fears of intrigue, riot, and sedition, always associated in his mind with popular elections. The only remedy, he said, was another constitutional convention to se- cure life or hereditary appointment of senators and a heredi- tary chief magistrate.[66] (He also called for amendments to make the veto power absolute and to strip the Senate of execu- tive functions.) Adams was not one to keep his opinions to himself; on the contrary, he flaunted them, and as his friend Mercy Warren said, the subject of his apostasy from repub- licanism "was viewed as a kind of political phenomenon."[67] Since his opinions of the new government were backed by three stout volumes of political philosophy, it was impossible to dismiss them as capricious. He claimed he was misrepresented and misunderstood. Perhaps he was, but "words are things," and if he meant to advocate only a dignified first magistracy and a high-toned senate, for instance, why did he use such volatile words as "monarchy" and "aristocracy" to describe them? Had he deliberately set out to make himself misun- derstood, he could not have succeeded better than he did.

Jefferson, certainly, believed that Adams had changed his opinions, and he deplored the change. In his mind, it need not affect their friendship, however, and so long as Adams' theories were encased in ponderous volumes few men had the fortitude to read, he was little concerned. But a faction of "monarchical federalists" centered in New York took up Adams and pushed him forward as the more or less innocent spokesman of their meditated designs.[68] Arriving in New York in March 1790, the watchwords of revolution fresh on his lips, Jefferson was struck with "wonder and mortification" by the conversation in the best circles of society. "Politics was the chief topic," he later recalled, "and a preference of kingly over republican government was evidently the favorite sentiment."[69] Falling in with this sentiment was a series of articles from Adams' pen which began to appear in the *Gazette of the United States*.[70] These *Discourses on Davila,* as they were named, continued the argument of the *Defence.* The historical analogies were drawn from a famous work on the French civil wars of the sixteenth century and pointed directly to the course of democracy in both France and the United States. The "passion for distinction" being the great spring of virtue and vice in human society, Adams said, the science of government might be reduced to the science of managing this passion for the public good. Ceremonies, ranks and titles compose one species of management, for the mass of mankind are children through life. But the fundamental principle of the science is the tripartite balance. Rejecting this principle, proceeding on "the wild idea of annihilating the nobility," the revolutionary government in France is destined to pass through the awful cycle of sedition and anarchy back to despotism. Equality is an illusion; the first rule of a well-balanced state, Adams suggested, is "that every man should know his place and be made to keep it."[71] No merely democratic government can long endure. Adams did not advocate the importation of kingship and nobility into the United States, but the tone of his argument and his use of these galvanizing abstractions made him an easy target of democratic opinion.

In May 1791 Jefferson was unwittingly thrust on the stage as

Adams' political antagonist, setting off an American version of the great debate in England between Edmund Burke and Thomas Paine on the French Revolution. Burke's *Reflections on the Revolution in France* appealed to conservative sentiments of order, tradition, religion, royalty, and privilege. It was read in the United States, of course, but so strong was the current of enthusiasm for the French Revolution that few men had the temerity to champion Burke's cause. Adams did not. Though he was rumored to have praised the *Reflections*,[72] he could not join Burke in mournful eulogy of the old regime or in hysterical denunciation of the revolution. The French were right in seeking to reform their institutions after the example of the Americans; Adams only regretted that they were so misguided in the attempt. Yet the spirit of the *Discourses on Davila* was not far removed from that of the *Reflections*. For Thomas Paine, Adams felt utter contempt. It is sometimes forgotten that Paine's vigorous reply to Burke, the first part of *The Rights of Man*, was at least inferentially an attack on John Adams as well. Paine assailed the English constitution and the theory of balanced government, which he ludicrously styled "a government of *this, that* and *t'other*," "a continual enigma," from which the American republic was mercifully free.[73] When Paine's pamphlet reached American shores, it was rushed into print and appeared, to Jefferson's chagrin, with a commendatory preface over his name. In this he expressed pleasure "that something was at length to be publicly said against the political heresies which had of late sprung up among us, not doubting that our citizens would rally again round the standard of Common Sense."[74] The preface was, in fact, a letter Jefferson had written transmitting the English copy of *The Rights of Man* to the printer in Philadelphia. He was dumbfounded when this casual piece of courtesy, appearing at the head of the pamphlet, placed him, the secretary of state, before the public not only as the champion of the French Revolution but as the denunciator of his old friend, the vice-president. For there was no mistaking Jefferson's veiled allusion to "political heresies." He meant the *Discourses on Davila*, as he candidly acknowledged to Washington. "I tell the writer [Adams] freely that he is a heretic, but certainly never meant to step into a public newspaper with that in my mouth."[75]

During the next two months the controversy between "Burkites and Painites," with Adams and Jefferson cast in tutelary roles, simmered and then came to a boil in the press. After Adams went home to Braintree in July, Jefferson addressed him a long letter. He explained the painful episode of the preface and said that nothing had been further from his intention than to drag either of their names before the public. "That you and I differ in our ideas of the best form of government is well known to us both; but we have differed as friends should do, respecting the purity of each other's motives, and confining our differences of opinion to private conversation."[76] Adams, in reply, credited Jefferson's motives but recounted in detail how the preface, with the pamphlet, had been construed as an "open personal attack" on him, holding him up to "the ridicule of the world for his meanness" and libeling him as the partisan of kings and nobles. With respect to political ideas, Adams was not aware that the two men had ever had a serious conversation on the subject; but if Jefferson supposed that he wished to introduce hereditary aristocracy and monarchy in the United States, he was mistaken. "It was high time," Adams concluded, "that you and I should come to an explanation with each other. The friendship that has subsisted for fifteen years between us without the smallest interruption, and until this occasion without the slightest suspicion, ever has been and still is, very dear to my heart."[77] Jefferson might better have left the matter there, but believing he was "as innocent in *effect* as . . . in intention," he sought to absolve himself completely. It was not his opinion of Paine's book that had set all the political tongues wagging, but the writings of one "Publicola," who in coming to the vice-president's defense had placed Jefferson in opposition to him.[78] Since "Publicola" was, in fact, young John Quincy Adams, this could not have gone down very well with the father. Even worse was Jefferson's denial that in alluding to "political heresies" he had had Adams in view. This little piece of mendacity, while meant to close the wound, had the opposite effect. Adams made no reply, nor would the two men correspond again for several years.

The friendship between Adams and Jefferson thus became a casualty of the French Revolution. Their little *contretemps* was part of a crowded political scene, but it accurately reflected the waxing ideological division in the American republic. Henceforth, though the problems of government might be as mundane as before, they were colored by the hopes and the fears, the affections and disaffections, the twin hysterias of exaltation and denunciation sent up in the progress of the French Revolution. Setting aside the personal embarrassment, Jefferson thought the controversy surrounding Paine's book proved salutary. It helped "to separate the wheat from the chaff." [79] It reawakened the spirit of 1776, underscored the relationship of principles and ideals between the two revolutions, and dramatized America's stake in the struggle for liberty abroad. In the office of secretary of state, Jefferson could not give full rein to his commitment to the French Revolution, but policy founded in the national interest, he believed, generally comported with that commitment. "I consider," he wrote, "the establishment and success of their government as necessary to stay up our own, and to prevent it from falling back to that kind of half-way house, the English constitution." He hoped "so beautiful a revolution" would "spread through the whole world." [80] And despite errors and excesses, despite the careers of exile and death that opened before many of his friends in Paris, Jefferson remained a champion of the French Revolution. Adams was astonished by the strength of Jefferson's commitment as well as by his growing partisanship. "There is not a Jacobin in France more devoted to faction," he wrote to Abigail in 1792.[81]

In later years he traced Jefferson's lapse to two erroneous opinions: first, "that Britain was tottering to her fall," and second, that France "would establish a free republican government and even a leveling democracy."[82] He had been taken in by the French philosophers, atheists all, madmen all—the true authors of the revolution, Adams thought—who preached liberty until they turned men into slaves, equality until they destroyed all justice, and fraternity until they cut each other's throats.[83]

Crushed by the weight of democratic opinion, run down as an aristocrat and monarchist, deserted by many of his former friends, Adams abruptly put away his pen, withdrew into the recesses of the vice-presidency, and fell silent in 1791. Within the administration he conducted himself as a loyal Federalist, while Jefferson became the favorite of the mushrooming Republican opposition. Many had seen Adams and Jefferson as the natural political rivals in the government under Washington. The rivalry did not develop, however, in part because of Adams' withdrawal, in part because of the old bond of friendship, but primarily because it was deflected by the conflict between Jefferson and Alexander Hamilton. Since neither of the old friends liked the upstart secretary of treasury, the rift between them was less severe than it might otherwise have been. Jefferson, for his part, placed Adams' heresies on a different plane from Hamilton's. Years afterwards he recalled a conversation between these men on the English constitution. "Purge that constitution of its corruption," Adams observed, "and give to its popular branch equality of representation, and it would be the most perfect ever devised by the wit of man." Hamilton returned, "Purge it of its corruption, and give to its popular branch equality of representation, and it would become an *impracticable* government: as it stands at present, with all its supposed defects, it is the most perfect government which ever existed."[84] This stated their differences exactly, Jefferson thought, with the addition that Adams was a monarchist in theory only, while Hamilton actually designed by corruption and force to transform the government after the English model. In the conflict between Jefferson and Hamilton, the question of the French Revolution merged with other issues of principle, interest, and power around which the first national political parties formed. But that is another story, superseding, and for a time silencing, the dialogue between Jefferson and Adams.

"The Revolution of 1800"

IN 1796 JOHN ADAMS AND THOMAS JEFFERSON WERE THE PRES-
idential candidates of the rival political parties that had grown
up during the past several years. Neither man was an advocate
of political parties as an instrument of government. The Constitution had been intended to function without them. Yet
political parties had formed on great issues of foreign and
domestic policy, each with its own array of doctrines, symbols,
and slogans, its own newspapers, its own network of alle-
giances—in outline, a system of two-party politics wholly
unknown to the official government of the Constitution. President George Washington issued a stern warning against the
"baneful" influence of parties in his farewell address. They
came between the people and their representatives, distracted
the public councils, agitated the community with ill-founded
jealousies and alarms, and were especially dangerous as channels of foreign intrigue in the young republic. Washington had
tried to govern as a leader above parties, and although he had
finally failed in this, becoming a Federalist president in spite of
himself, the almost universal veneration for his name had been
a unifying force, perhaps the strongest the country possessed.
With his retirement this force would be removed, for no national halo surrounded Adams or Jefferson or anyone else.
Extreme partisanship would likely assert itself and the transition prove difficult whoever the new president might be.

The presidential campaign tended to confirm these appre-
hensions. Following on the heels of the divisive Jay Treaty, the
campaign featured Federalists and Republicans trading ac-

cusations of subversion to foreign influence, the former, as
friends of the treaty, to Great Britain, the latter, its ardent foes,
to France. In this great division in foreign affairs—one that
went back to the American Revolution but matured in the
French Revolution and the subsequent war between the
monarchical coalition, Britain at the head, and the French
republic—Adams and Jefferson were clearly identified in the
public mind as the friends of Britain and France respectively.
The French Revolution had become a political touchstone,
communicating to American politics the passions, the hopes
and fears, of a struggle between revolutionary and counter-
revolutionary forces in the Western world. Not only had the
vice-president supported the British treaty, as he had all the
leading measures of the Washington administration, but he
was also remembered for his advocacy of doctrines favorable to
monarchy and aristocracy and hostile to the democratic revolution. (The libelous use made of the *Defence of the American
Constitutions* during the campaign, he remarked, gave him no
pain, since it caused the book to be read by more people during
six months than would otherwise read it in a hundred years.) [1]
Republicans portrayed Adams as "the champion of rank, titles
and hereditary distinctions," while Jefferson was imaged as
"the steadfast friend to the rights of the people." [2]

The Federalists, of course, had no use for Jefferson, and in
the inner circle around Alexander Hamilton, the former secretary of treasury, there was little enthusiasm for Adams. It
was Hamilton who, unknown to Adams, had schemed to throw
votes away from him upon his election as vice-president; and in
1796 Hamilton secretly plotted to bring in another Federalist
candidate, Thomas Pinckney, over Adams' head. The Hamiltonians considered Adams vain, jealous, and independent. He
was not one of them. Despite the Jay Treaty, he frowned at
Britain; despite the favorite Federalist measures to stimulate a
capitalistic economy, he hated banks and paper money, prized
social order over innovation and growth, and seemed to share

the simple "agrarian" preferences of the Jeffersonians.[3] Obsessed with ideas of his own dignity, and conceiving of the first magistracy as a stewardship of the national interest, loftily ruling over "the spirit of party," Adams, the Hamiltonians feared, would make a fetish of his independence and brook no interference from them. Yet they had little choice but to take him in 1796. He had been a good soldier in the second office, at least since 1791; his private character was unassailable; and he had more political assets and fewer liabilities than any other available Federalist. On the whole, his claims to the succession could not be denied.

Jefferson had left the government at the end of 1793 with resolutions of never again stirring from his beloved Monticello. "My farm, my family and my books call me to them irresistibly," he said.[4] Before long he was boasting of never reading a newspaper. To these resolutions his Republican friends quietly demurred, while the Federalists suspected they covered a political ambition so poisonous Jefferson dared not acknowledge it to himself. Adams never doubted that the Virginian, for all his vauntings of philosophical tranquility, was his principal rival. Far from being "the ardent pursuer of science" that some thought him, Jefferson was so indolent and so consumed by politics that he would die of frustration at Monticello, Adams predicted. His retirement was, in fact, a masterful political stroke to gain the presidency. "Jefferson thinks by this step to get a reputation as an humble, modest, meek man, wholly without ambition or vanity. He may even have deceived himself into this belief. But if the prospect opens, the world will see and he will feel that he is as ambitious as Oliver Cromwell."[5] History would bear Adams out. Yet there is no reason to question the sincerity of Jefferson's earlier professions. The Jay Treaty shook him out of his political slumber at Monticello. Viewing it as the capstone of the Hamiltonian system, Jefferson said it was "nothing more than a treaty of alliance between England and the Anglomen of this country against . . . the people of the United States."[6] Nevertheless, he had no wish to return to the political wars. "The little spice of ambition which I had in my younger days has long since evaporated," he told Madison, the Republican leader and his personal candidate.[7] He never consented to run, or if elected to serve; and lest he refuse, he was not even asked. It had all been done against his will, Jefferson protested. If his friends believed him, it was too much to expect of his enemies. Wasn't it marvelous, Adams quipped, how political plants grew in the shade![8]

The two candidates were silent observers of the campaign that raged around them, and neither could truthfully recognize the other in the images limned by partisan foes. They had, after Jefferson's departure from Philadelphia, occasionally exchanged letters, which showed how reluctant each man was to yield the old friendship and yet, at the same time, the difficulty of maintaining it on the condition of evading the questions that concerned them most. Thus when Jefferson introduced his idea of the sovereign right of each living generation to determine its destiny independently of its predecessors—an idea inspired by the French Revolution—Adams checked himself, returning only a mild dissent, and Jefferson dropped the subject so obviously harrowing to Adams' feelings.[9] The next letters between them came six months later. And so it went. Early in the election year, months before it was known for certain that Washington would retire, Adams hinted at his own retirement, hoping in this way to sound the depths of Jefferson's ambition. In a masterful reply, the latter again expressed his loathing of politics, signaled his confidence in Adams' republicanism and implied he would never be an obstacle in his way. "I am sure, from the honesty of your heart," he wrote, "you join me in detestation of the corruption of the English government, and that no man on earth is more incapable than yourself of seeing that copied among us, willingly. I have been among those who have feared the design to introduce it here, and it has been a strong reason with me for wishing there was an ocean of fire between that government and us. But away with politics."[10] The final flourish had become such a cliché that it no longer carried conviction, certainly not to Adams, though he was reassured by Jefferson's sentiments in regard to himself. Adams could not pretend to an indifference he did not feel; he desperately wanted to be president of the United States and was determined to play second fiddle to no one but Washington.

Jefferson, on the other hand, if he must serve, preferred the second office to the first. The electoral vote was uncomfortably close (the final tally showed 71 for Adams, 68 for Jefferson) and while it was still undecided he wrote to Madison that in case of a tie the decision in the House of Representatives should go to Adams.[11] He had always been senior. Defeat would cost Jefferson nothing; it would cost Adams everything. Besides, the vice-presidency was "honorable and easy," affording him "philosophical evenings in the winter, and rural days in the summer," while the presidency was but "splendid misery." Finally, the storm that had been brewing with France was about to burst upon the nation, and now was not the time for a Republican to take the helm. Madison quietly circulated his friend's letter in Philadelphia, where it fell in with the sentiments other Republicans were receiving from Monticello, and raised the possibility of a political entente between moderate Federalists and Republicans. Adams seemed cordial. As Madison and others reported, he spoke of Jefferson in friendly terms and invited a conciliatory administration in cooperation with him.[12] Hamiltonian Federalists were alarmed. It was all a "Jacobinical intrigue" to divide the party, and Adams was lending himself to the plot. "Our Jacobins say they are well pleased," Hamilton wrote in disgust, "and that the *Lion* and the *Lamb* are to lie down together. Mr Adams' *personal* friends talk a little the same way. Mr. *Jefferson* is not half so ill a man as we have been accustomed to think him. There is to be a vigorous and united administration. . . . If Mr. Adams has *Vanity*," he concluded, " 'tis plain a plot has been laid to take hold of it." [13]

There was no plot, yet Hamilton's suspicions were well founded. While the prospects of political concord matured in Philadelphia, Jefferson wrote a warm, congratulatory letter to Adams. No one could congratulate him with more disinterestedness, he said. Though he might not be believed, he had never for a moment wished for his own election. "I have no ambition to govern men. It is a painful and thankless office. Since the day too when you signed the treaty of Paris our horizon was never so overcast." He prayed that Adams' administration would be "filled with glory and happiness to yourself and advantage to us," issued a pointed warning against "the subtlety of your arch-friend of New York," Hamilton, and pledged his support.[14] It was obvious that Adams would have to seek support either from the ultras in his own party or from the Republicans. In Jefferson's view, the mass of Federalists were, like Adams, republicans at heart who had been misled by the Hamiltonians and seduced by the popularity of Washington. The latter influence had been withdrawn and the former might be checked. Jefferson hoped to draw Adams and the moderates into the Republican party, or rather into a grand political consensus that would render parties and their dissensions insignificant. He worried over the letter to Adams, discouraged by the difficulty of making himself believed, and laid it aside. After reading the reports of Adams' friendly attitude, he decided to send the letter, but, still hesitant, put it under cover of another to Madison, who was authorized to intercept or forward this epistle from Monticello as his on-the-spot judgment in Philadelphia dictated. "If Mr. Adams can be induced to administer the government on its true principles, and to relinquish his bias to an English constitution," Jefferson said, "it is to be considered whether it would not be on the whole for the public good to come to an understanding with him." [15]

Madison was startled by the suggestion of an understanding, probably a coalition; and if this was the kind of overture that lurked in the honeyed phrases of Jefferson's letter, it should go no farther. And it did not. Madison was still no friend of Adams, but his action was based on hard political calculations. The conciliatory feelings between Adams and Jefferson were well enough advertised already, he argued. Any excessive forwardness on Jefferson's part would compromise his independence and prove embarrassing should the course of the new administration call for vigorous opposition. Nor should the interests of the youthful Republican party, only now beginning to feel its strength, be neglected. Already many Republicans groaned at the idea of a rapprochement. Adams had everything to gain by it, the Republicans everything to lose. The true policy, Madison said, lay in cultivating Adams' better nature, separating him from the ultras, and giving a fair start to his executive career without, however, in any way compromising the integrity of the Republican party. Jefferson was persuaded. He thanked his friend for suppressing the overture, and on this note the dialogue on conciliation was adjourned, to be resumed a few weeks later upon Jefferson's arrival in Philadelphia.[16]

The mounting crisis with France stared Adams in the face at the outset of his administration. The French Directory, angry over the Jay Treaty, had retaliated by plundering America's neutral commerce and had even made a clumsy attempt to influence the outcome of the presidential election. Diplomatic relations between the two countries had collapsed. Several months previous, Washington had recalled James Monroe for alleged failure to cushion the shock of the Jay Treaty in Paris. The Directory then turned its back on Monroe's replacement, Charles Cotesworth Pinckney. Jefferson believed that Hamilton and his minions in Washington's cabinet, which the new president was about to inherit, would attempt to use the crisis to provoke war with France in alliance with Britain. Adams might avert this calamity. Jefferson did not think that he wanted war. He had, to be sure, backed the pro-British foreign policy of Washington's second administration; but Jefferson remembered his earlier preachments favorable to American "disentanglement" from Europe, antagonistic to Britain, and at least acquiescent in the French alliance. On March 3, the day before his inauguration, Adams called on Jefferson to discuss a bipartisan approach to the French crisis. Writing of the interview some years later, Adams said, "Though by this time I differed from him [Jefferson] in opinion by the whole horizon concerning the practicality and success of the French Revolution, and some other points, I had no reason to think that he differed materially from me with regard to our national Constitution. I did not think that the rumbling voice of party calumny ought to discourage me from consulting [one] whom I knew to be attached to the interest of the nation, and whose experience, genius, learning, and travels had eminently qualified him to give advice." [17] Adams' first wish was to send Jefferson to France. The same idea had occurred to several of Adams' friends, who saw it in the same light as he did, as a way of accommodating the prejudices and opinions of the Republicans. But Jefferson said he was sick of Europe and would never think of going there again. Even had his response been different, Adams thought the government would be degraded by the dispatch of the "crown prince" on a diplomatic mission. He then unfolded the plan of a bipartisan commission. Various names were mentioned, but Madison was the key to its success. Would he go? Jefferson agreed to ask him. As expected, Madison declined. On March 6, as he and Adams walked back to their lodgings following a farewell dinner at Washington's table, Jefferson reported the result of his inquiry. Adams, somewhat embarrassed, said he had already dropped the idea. He did not explain why, but Jefferson suspected what had happened. When Adams had mentioned Madison's name to one of the cabinet officers, Oliver Wolcott, secretary of treasury, he was met with the pouting response, "Mr. President, we are willing to resign."[18] The ultra-Federalists, Adams discovered, would not tolerate the conciliatory gesture he had planned, and rather than fight them, he submitted. As Jefferson remembered that evening stroll with Adams, they came to the point "where our road separated . . . and we took leave; and he never after that said one word to me on the subject [of the French mission] or ever consulted me as to any measure of the government."[19] It was a momentous parting, full of consequences for the government of the United States.

The euphoria of reconciliation still lingered after Adams' inaugural address. There were things in it that must have jarred Jefferson. Considered in the abstract, "the spirit of party" and "the pestilence of foreign influence" were indeed dangers to free government; but why did Adams feel compelled to introduce these condemnatory phrases, so long hurled at the Republicans, into his address? And what was his perfervid resolution to appoint only good Christians to office but a slap at Jefferson and his philosophical friends? More importantly, however, Adams declared his unequivocal loyalty to the Constitution, repelling the "political heresies" that had been charged to him, and professed his friendship for the French nation.[20] Republicans were pleased with the address, while some Federalists thought it "temporizing." But the euphoria soon vanished. Adams made the decision to retain Washington's cabinet: Timothy Pickering, Oliver Wolcott, and James McHenry, all high Federalists who took their marching orders from Hamilton. Adams refused to credit the stories of Hamilton's "Pinckney plot" in 1796 and, of course, did not suspect the extent of the New Yorker's influence over his chief advisers. He bowed to the party yoke without knowing he was putting it on. The implications were plain to Jefferson on March 6. Every effort would be made to keep foreign policy on a collision course with France and also to alienate the president from him. As events unfolded, Jefferson realized how mistaken he had been to seek a political accommodation with Adams. He gave himself over to the Federalists, yet, what was worse, imagined himself the lofty and lonely sentinel of the national interest. Washington had made the delusion believable, almost to the end, but Adams was no Washington and the president who attempted to repeat his performance was doomed to disappointment.

Adams convened a special session of Congress in May to deal with the French crisis. Recent dispatches from Pinckney, the president declared, proved the determination of the French government to force its will on the United States by a combination of plunder, insult, and blackmail. He did not call for an immediate declaration of war but for strong defense measures to back up the commission he intended to send to France in a last effort to preserve peace.[21] Nevertheless, Jefferson and the Republicans heard the speech as a "war message." The plan to negotiate peace while preparing for war was a transparent fraud. Peace being the great imperative of the nation, in Jefferson's opinion, the crisis called for a posture of conciliation rather than of sword-rattling insult and recrimination. He did not believe France wanted war with the United States, though she might be provoked to it by the "British faction" that had thrown American commerce into the scales of British power and then treated French protests with contempt, as by the recall of Monroe and now by Adams' blustering speech. British monopoly and influence still held the country in bondage, Jefferson thought. What was amazing was that the British faction, by raising the hue and cry of "foreign influence," had been able "so far to throw dust into the eyes of our citizens, as to fix on those who wish merely to recover self-government the charge of subserving one foreign influence, because they resist submission to another."[22] He was reluctant to include the president in the British faction, yet his policy seemed to place him there. And, in fact, Adams did now believe that France was the mortal enemy of the United States, less from her weight in

the European balance of power than from her zeal in foment-
ing revolution abroad, seizing on popular notions of democracy, separating the people from their government, and turning demagogic leaders into traitors against their own country.
This system of revolutionary terror had conquered Holland
and Geneva and was raising havoc all over Europe. Who could
doubt that the French Directory practiced the same system
toward the United States? Of course a "French party" existed;
it began with the alliance of 1778, nourished itself on weak
ideas of national gratitude and British malignity, and grew into
a monster on the popular heresy that the French Revolution
was an extension of the American. Adams was determined that
France would not "put petticoats" on the United States, as she
had on others. And if war should result, it would not be the
worst of dangers. War upheld honor, and it had, at least, heroic
virtues, which were not unwanted in a torpid "bedollared
nation." [23]

By the end of the special session of Congress, the political
break between Adams and Jefferson was complete. The appointment of a three-man commission temporarily defused
the crisis. Jefferson was satisfied with the commission primarily
because of the inclusion of Elbridge Gerry, of Massachusetts, a
moderate Federalist who had been acting as a self-appointed
mediator between him and Adams. Gerry kept relaying Jefferson's reassuring words to Adams only to find them cancelled by
the machinations of the Hamiltonians who surrounded him.
"It cannot help but damp the pleasure of cordiality, when we
suspect that it is suspected," Jefferson remarked to Gerry in
May. "I cannot help fearing, that it is impossible for Mr. Adams
to believe that the state of my mind is what it really is, that he
may think I view him as an obstacle in my way." [24] This is
precisely what Adams concluded, and not without reason.
Jefferson, who had expected his office to be "honorable and
easy," was thrust into another and unofficial role, the leadership of the Republican party, in which he was the second most

powerful figure in the country. The vice-presidency, Federalists came to believe, was a privileged sanctuary from which Jefferson conducted a partisan campaign against the government. What a travesty on the office of the "crown prince"! Adams had given loyal support to President Washington; it was, he said, "the pride and boast" of his life, and he had hoped that Jefferson, placed in the same office, would conduct himself in the same dignified manner.[25] Instead he surrounded himself with pernicious political characters, threw off all restraints on ambition, aimed to pull Adams down by fair means or foul, and mount to the presidency on the ruins of his administration.

Duplicity, ultra-Federalists had argued, was the fundamental vice of Jefferson's character, and Adams became convinced he was an object of it. Publication in May of the Virginian's year-old letter to Philip Mazzei disclosed the extent of his malignity, not only to the ruling Federalists, who were denounced as "an Anglican monarchical and aristocratical party," but also to Washington, elliptically lumped with apostates "who have had their heads shorn by the harlot England."[26] If these were Jefferson's true sentiments toward his predecessor, Adams could not help but wonder what they were toward him. In June an old friend, Uriah Forrest, forwarded the evidence that turned suspicions into certainties. Forrest had been privy to certain "disgraceful insinuations" and "barefaced assertions" Jefferson had made in a confidential letter to a Maryland Republican. Struck by the discrepancy between the censorious tone of the letter and the public professions of cordiality to Adams, Forrest thought the president should be put on guard. The revelation was "a serious thing," he replied. "It is evidence of a mind, soured, yet seeking for popularity, and eaten to a honeycomb with ambition, yet weak, confused, uninformed, and ignorant."[27] The breech with Jefferson was irrevocable, Adams soon reported to his son. "You can witness for me how loath I have been to give him up. It is with much reluctance that I am obliged to look upon him as a man whose mind is warped by prejudice and so blinded by ignorance as to be unfit for the office he holds. However wise and scientific as a philosopher, as a politician he is a child and the dupe of party!" [28] Without reciprocating the personal acrimony, Jefferson thought it was Adams who had become "the dupe of party."

The breech, for all its historical and human interest, assumed much greater significance as in the course of events Adams and Jefferson came to stand for fundamentally incompatible conceptions of political freedom in the American republic. The road to the "revolution of 1800," which brought Jefferson to the presidency, passed through the "crisis of 1798" and took its character as a consequence. The outcome of the mission to France became known in April, when Congress published the dispatches of the envoys detailing the so-called XYZ Affair: the intrigue by agents of the French foreign office to secure a large loan and douceur as the price of treating with the Americans. The nation was outraged. Jefferson made the best excuses he could for France, rallied the wavering Republicans, and argued strenuously for keeping the door open to peace. Adams' immediate reaction had been to demand a declaration of war, but he drew back and settled for an accelerated defense program, meanwhile letting opinion ripen for war. Congress proceeded to renounce the French treaties, suspend trade, build frigates, authorize the capture of French ships, lay direct taxes, and establish a large provisional army. Under cover of the whipped-up war hysteria, the Federalists assailed the patriotism of the Republicans and portrayed the more zealous among them as Jacobin disorganizers in the country's bowels, whose ultimate treachery only awaited the signal of the French invaders.

"Whatever chance was left of escaping war after the publication of the dispatches," Jefferson wrote in May, "the President's answers to the addresses pouring in on him from the great towns . . . are pushing the irritation to a point to which nobody can expect it will be bourne."[29] These bombastic answers revealed a style of thinking, even a political philosophy, sharply at odds with Jefferson's. Adams denounced the "rage for innovation," which had been raised to a "pitch of madness" by "the wild philosophy" of the French Revolution, and which had nothing in common with the conservative wisdom of the American.[30] Jefferson was no longer enthralled by the French Revolution, but he still believed in the ideals that had inspired it and in the Enlightenment directive to learn from the follies rather than the alleged wisdom of the past. Adams appealed to the religious feelings of the people in behalf of the war spirit, proclaimed national fast days, and contended that religious duty was a necessary postulate of republican government.[31] Jefferson held that the duties of religion were of no concern to the state, and after he became president declined to proclaim fast days. Adams lashed out at the "spirit of party, which scruples not to go all lengths of profligacy, falsehood, and malignity in defaming our government."[32] What was this, Jefferson asked himself, but a denial of any title of patriotism to Republican opponents of the administration? What was it but the bold assertion that those who censured the governors attacked the government itself? "Nor is it France alone," he observed, "but his own fellow citizens against whom his threats are uttered."[33] Decrying "domestic treachery" more fatal than war, Adams supposed that war may have been sent by Providence to extinguish the evil. There were no greater enemies than those who still pled the cause of France or paralyzed the vengeance of the government. To the "soldier-citizens" of New Jersey he stoutly declared that "the degraded and deluded characters may tremble, lest they should be condemned to the severest punishment an American suffers—that of being conveyed in safety within the lines of an invading enemy."[34] No one could doubt for whom these grotesqueries were intended. It was enough to plunge Jefferson's friend Madison into mel-

ancholy reflection on the old truth, which perhaps not even the
most favored nation on God's footstool would escape, "that the
loss of liberty at home is to be charged to provisions against
dangers real or pretended abroad." [35]

Adams entered heart and soul into the war hysteria. On May
7 the "Young Men of Philadelphia," twelve hundred strong,
the black cockade in their hats (a counter-symbol to the tricol-
ored cockade) paraded down Market Street to a swelling
throng before the president's house. They came to offer their
lives if need be in war against France. Adams received them in
full military regalia, heard their address, and responded with a
lecture on ancestral piety that proved to be especially grating to
Jefferson. The American Revolution had arisen not from dis-
content, not to effect anything new in government, Adams
declared, but "to vindicate the immemorial liberties of our
ancestors." [36] Two days later, on the national fast day, rumors
spread of a Jacobin plot to terrorize the city. A few scuffles
occurred, a sham battle of the cockades, and the lighthorse
patrolled the streets that night, but nothing more disturbing to
the public peace. Fifteen years afterwards, Adams freely recalled the spectacle for Jefferson: "When . . . Market Street was
as full as men could stand by one another, and even before my
door; when some of my domestics, in frenzy, determined to
sacrifice their lives in my defense . . . ; when I myself judged it
prudent and necessary to order chests of arms from the War
Office, to be brought through by lanes and back doors; determined to defend my house at the expense of my life. . . . What
think you of terrorism, Mr. Jefferson?" [37] Jefferson, whom
Adams supposed had been "fast asleep in philosophical tranquility," thought in 1813, as in 1798, that the terrorism had
come from the Federalist "war party," yet the delusion of a
Jacobin conspiracy still hung in the old man's memory.

This little bit of retrospection was started by Adams when he
discovered that Jefferson had criticized his address to the
young Philadelphians as an appeal to the past against the

progress of science. It was an issue to which Jefferson was
especially sensitive. As a good *philosophe*, he thought that a
country, a government, dedicated to the freedom and happiness of the people ought to cherish the methods with the fruits
of scientific inquiry. Science and freedom were coupled in his
thinking. His ideal was not merely a democratic republic but "a
republic of science," and he spoke of freedom as "the first born
daughter of science," thereby linking the political revolution of
his age with the scientific revolution earlier commenced by
Copernicus and Galileo. Freedom of inquiry was the beginning
of political freedom; the latter could not exist without the
former. Yet Federalist spokesmen constantly ridiculed Jefferson's scientific pretensions and accused him of "philoso-
phism"—an *ism* that combined the qualities of infidelity,
pedantry, and dreamy utopianism, all unwanted in the practical business of statecraft. "It suffices," Jefferson wrote indignantly in 1798, "for a man to be a philosopher, and to believe
that human affairs are susceptible to improvement, and to look
forward, rather than back to Gothic ages, for perfection, to
mark him as an anarchist, disorganizer, atheist and enemy of
the government." [38] Adams, of course, had no idea of going
back to "Gothic ages," yet Jefferson thought the tendency of
Federalist doctrine justified the charge, hyperbole and all. In
his conception of the party conflict, and of the choice before
the people in 1800, he and the Republicans stood for "the
progress of science," Adams and the Federalists "for awing the
human mind with stories of raw-head and bloody bones to the
distrust of its own vision." [39] The issue was philosophical, between the friends· and enemies of enlightenment, therefore
elevated far above the usual petty quarrels of politicians. It was
this conviction that had prompted his criticism of Adams'
addresses, Jefferson wrote in retrospect. "One of the questions
you know on which our parties took different sides, was on the
improvability of the human mind, in science, in ethics, in
government etc. Those who advocated reformation of institu-

tions, pari passu, with the progress of science, maintained that
no definite limit could be assigned to that progress. The
enemies of reform, on the other hand, denied improvement,
and advocated steady adherence to the principles, practices
and institutions of our fathers, which they represented as the
consummation of wisdom, and acme of excellence, beyond
which the human mind could never advance."[40]

The issue assumed most tangible form in the Alien and
Sedition Laws of 1798. The former was but one of three laws
enacted against aliens; the other two lengthened the period of
residence required for citizenship from five to fourteen years
and regulated the status of enemy aliens in time of war. The
Alien (or Alien Friends) Law authorized the president sum-
marily to deport aliens deemed dangerous to the peace and
safety of the United States. As originally passed by the Senate,
over which he presided, Jefferson thought it "worthy of the
eighth or ninth century;" and he did not think much better of
the final act.[41] It was aimed at two large foreign-born groups,
the French and the Irish, who were allegedly arrayed on the
side of the malcontents, and more particularly at certain philosophers and journalists: Joseph Priestley, Thomas Cooper,
C. F. Volney, William Duane, and others who were Jefferson's
friends and associates. The Sedition Act, aimed at "domestic
traitors," made it a federal crime punishable by fine and im-
prisonment to publish "any false, scandalous and malicious
writing" against the government, Congress, or the president.
The act rested on the ancient rule of law that government, and
governors, can be criminally assaulted by opinion and, further,
that government has an inherent right to protect itself, indeed
to protect the people themselves whose guardians the governors are, by punishing so-called seditious libels. Jefferson had
predicted passage of a sedition law weeks before the subject
was introduced in Congress. The president's addresses invited
it; the rising intolerance of any opinion critical of the war
system demanded it. The real object of the law, which the

smokescreen of Jacobin intrigue and subversion could not conceal, was the suppression of the Republican press.

The French crisis precipitated the Sedition Law, but viewed in the longer perspective of political controversy, Jefferson could see it as the more or less inevitable outcome of Federalist ideology. Conceiving of themselves as a ruling class, as the guardians of the government they had established, the Federalist leaders feared its vulnerability to the shifting currents of public opinion, feared the "natural turbulence" of the populace, and denied the legitimacy of a political opposition organized outside the official channels of the Constitution. When the Jeffersonians went outside the government and built a political party in the broad electorate, they set up a different ideal, one that saw in the agitation and mobilization of public opinion the vital principle of republican government. The people were to be cherished, not feared; the free criticism of "constituted authorities," so long condemned, became a political virtue; and the government was no longer to check, control, or rise above public opinion but to merge with it.

The issue was never far from the surface during the Federalist decade. In 1791 Jefferson and Madison set in motion a newspaper, the *National Gazette*, intended to counteract the court newspaper in the capital and to circulate throughout the country as "a Whig vehicle of intelligence." The proposition behind this move had been clearly enunciated by Jefferson. As the people are "the only censors of their governors," it is necessary to give them full information of public affairs; newspapers penetrating "the whole mass of the people" are the surest means to this end. "The basis of our governments being the opinion of the people," he said, "the very first object should be to keep that right; and were it left to me to decide whether we should have a government without newspapers, or newspapers without a government, I should not hesitate a moment to prefer the latter."[42] The Federalist leaders, Hamilton at the front, felt threatened by the *National Gazette* and launched a

campaign to discredit it as a tool of faction tending to subvert
the government. In 1793 the country witnessed a spontaneous
outburst of "democratic societies," similar to the correspond-
ing societies before the American Revolution, though their
impetus was another revolution, the French, and they sought
to channel enthusiasm for revolution abroad into the Republican cause at home. The Federalists linked the societies to the
notorious Jacobin Clubs of Paris and implicated them in the
Whiskey Rebellion of 1794. President Washington then delivered the crushing blow by publicly condemning them as illicit
political engines. Jefferson was shocked: "It is wonderful indeed, that the President should have permitted himself to be
the organ of such an attack on the freedom of discussion, the
freedom of writing, printing and publishing."[43] Two years
later, in his farewell address, Washington again betrayed intolerance of political opposition from outside constituted channels of authority. Unknown to Jefferson, Adams' opinion was,
if anything, more severe. The democratic societies were "criminal" he said, as it was unlawful "to meet and publish censures
upon laws and libels upon men and measures."[44] More recently, in 1797, the grand jury of the federal circuit court at
Richmond, presided over by an associate justice of the Supreme Court, issued a presentment against Virginia congressman Samuel J. Cabell for disseminating in letters to his
constituents "unfounded calumnies against the happy government of the United States." Jefferson at once demanded
protective action by the Virginia assembly.[45]

The Alien and Sedition Laws originated with the Federalist
leaders in Congress, yet Adams bore a substantial share of
responsibility for them. He helped to create the climate of
opinion in which they were enacted; he articulated the principles and fears they embodied; and despite later disclaimers, he
cooperated in their enforcement. The Alien Law was not fully
executed in a single instance, primarily because the more
celebrated of the "degraded foreigners," as Adams called

them, took the first ship out of the country. But Adams signed blank warrants for Secretary of State Pickering and specifically authorized him to expel at least three aliens. Moreover, he denied passports to certain foreigners, one of them Jefferson's friend Dupont de Nemours, supposedly on a scientific mission but suspected of spying for the Directory. "We have had too many French philosophers already," Adams told Pickering, "and I really begin to think . . . that learned academics, not under the immediate inspection and control of government, have disorganized the world, and are incompatible with social order."[46] Quite aside from his taste for French philosophers, Jefferson, from his first publication, the *Summary View*, had advocated the natural right of expatriation, which, by reciprocity, denied the right of exclusion to any country. Federalists, on the other hand, tended to follow the common-law rule of perpetual allegiance. The Sedition Law, unlike the Alien Law, was generously enforced. Twenty-five persons were arrested, fourteen indicted, ten tried and ten convicted, principally Republican printers and publicists. Most of the prosecutions were targeted for political effect. Scarcely an opposition newspaper north of the Potomac escaped this "reign of terror." Jefferson's forecast for the law was thus amply fulfilled.

Congress finally adjourned in July, and the president and vice-president returned to their homes. Surprisingly, war had not been declared, though almost every leading Federalist, including the president, had favored it to the ambiguous "quasi-war"—a war of frigates and privateers—then existing. During the long summer and fall, the gloomiest of his life, he said, Adams was in poor health, his wife seriously ill, and the reins of control over his administration slipped from his grasp. Ironically, the advocate in theory of a "monarchical" executive proved to be a weak president. He lost a crucial contest with the cabinet over the second command, second to Washington, of the provisional army. The post went to Hamilton, who had ambitious plans for employing the army together with the

British fleet in conquest of Spanish dominions. This was dismaying enough to Adams, and when combined with his ancient Whig prejudice against standing armies, it definitely cooled his ardor for war. "If this nation sees a great army to maintain, without an enemy to fight," he wrote to Secretary of War McHenry in October, "there may arise an enthusiasm that seems to be little foreseen. At present, there is no more prospect of seeing a French army here, than there is in Heaven." [47] The navy, on the other hand, partly because it was not an engine of domestic repression, had Adams' blessing.

Jefferson seemed confident when he returned to Monticello that the evils of standing army, debt and taxes, and oppressive laws would produce their own cure. "A little patience, and we shall see the reign of witches pass over, their spells dissolved, and the people recovering their true sight, restoring the government to its true principles." [48] After two or three months, however, he decided that some incantations by the Republicans were wanted to break the spell. The delusion of the people was so necessary to the Federalists, there was no limit to which they might not go. Would the Republican party survive? Would the republic itself survive? The Alien and Sedition Laws, the worst atrocities thus far, appeared to Jefferson as "merely an experiment on the American mind" to see to what degradation it would submit. "If this goes down," he said, recalling older fears, "we shall immediately see attempted another act of Congress, declaring that the President shall continue in office during life, reserving to another occasion the transfer of the succession to his heir, and the establishment of the Senate for life." [49] Among the lesser possibilities of 1798 was that of John Adams, for all his momentary popularity, being declared president for life. To such chimeras had the "terror of '98" carried the leader of the Republican party. Still, in view of the Federalist monopoly of all branches of the government including the judiciary, almost anything was possible. A "revolution of opinion" was necessary, and Jefferson chose to start it in two Republican state legislatures.

The Kentucky and Virginia resolutions of 1798, the former secretly drafted by Jefferson, the latter by Madison, declared the Alien and Sedition Laws unconstitutional and appealed to the other states to do likewise.[50] Jefferson's resolutions set forth the theory of the Union as a compact among the several states. Acts beyond the delegated powers of the federal government were void, and there being no ultimate arbiter of the Constitution, each state had a right to judge for itself the infractions as well as the mode and measure of redress. The Alien and Sedition Laws were found to be gross usurpations of power, therefore warranting the action of "nullification" by state authority. Freedom of speech and press had the same standing under the First Amendment as freedom of religion, Jefferson argued. Congress could legislate in no matter whatever. He did not enter a broadly philosophical plea for these freedoms, preferring rather to rest the case on constitutional grounds, which he considered unassailable. The limits of state authority over these freedoms were left undefined and undisturbed. This did no harm in 1798 when the danger came from the federal government; and Jefferson's theoretical commitment to freedom of speech and press was hardly open to question. Much more serious, and open to question, was the appeal to state legislatures to adjudge, arrest, or "nullify" a federal law. This raised the specter of disunion, a cure likely to prove no less fatal than the disease. But whatever the later significance of these famous resolutions for the issue of state rights and union—the constitutional issue on which the Civil War would be fought—they originated in a struggle for political survival and addressed the fundamental issue of freedom and self-government descending from the American Revolution.

Adams doubtless considered the Virginia and Kentucky res-

olutions sedition itself, though he seems not to have suspected
Jefferson's responsibility for them. His ideas of the scope of
national power under the Constitution were fully as broad as
Hamilton's, and he abhorred state rights doctrines whether
they came from the Republicans or, at a later time, from the
Federalists. At home in Quincy he was bombarded with letters
and reports conveying assurances of the French government's
desire to reopen negotiations with the United States. While
they were not without effect, Adams' annual message to Congress in December, stiffened by Hamiltonian influence in the
cabinet, proposed no relaxation of the administration's warlike
posture. Then, on February 18, 1799, without forewarning or
consultation, the president nominated William Vans Murray,
the American envoy at The Hague, as minister plenipotentiary
to negotiate peace with France. The Federalist leaders were
outraged. "Never did a party show stronger mortification,"
Jefferson wrote, "and, consequently, that war had been their
object." [51] Jefferson should have been overjoyed. But he was
unable to accept the nomination at face value. Nothing in
Adams' recent conduct suggested that he was any less in-
fatuated with the war system than the ultras in his party. On the
very day of Murray's nomination, the army bill looking to a
force of 30,000 regulars and 75,000 volunteers cleared the
Senate for the president's signature. Some days earlier, the
Senate had approved his nomination of envoys to negotiate
treaties of amity and commerce with Russia and Turkey, both
new accessions to the second coalition against France. What
was this, Jefferson wondered, but a deliberate provocation to
get from France the declaration of war the administration was
afraid to be the first in making? Adams had gone on inflaming
the public mind with his addresses. The domestic machinery of
the war system remained in place. Although petitions poured
into Congress begging the repeal of the Alien and Sedition
Laws, the Federalist majority specifically reaffirmed them.
Moreover, the administration stepped up enforcement of the

Sedition Law, keeping the gun at Republican heads throughout the ensuing presidential election. All considered, then,
Jefferson had reason to be skeptical of the Murray mission. He
conjectured that Adams, finding he could no longer conceal
French advances, took a step "which would parry the overture
while it wears the face of acceding to it." The president expected the Senate to reject the nomination of Murray, he
supposed; and if it did not the administration would effectively
negate the mission by tactics of obstruction and delay.[52]

Jefferson was wrong, in the main. It was a pity he could not
perceive the irony of the situation. Adams plunged a sword
into the Federalist party, one which its leaders believed a be-
trayal to Jeffersonianism, but which appeared to Jefferson as
only a "parry" of French advances. He had forgotten that John
Adams, whatever else he was, was an honest man and a man
ultimately driven, even perversely driven, to self-righteous
independence of party. Rather than risk all character for pro-
bity, he would make the stretch for a peace he did not expect or
perhaps want. Even as he nominated Murray, he voiced contempt for "the babyish and womanly blubbering for peace,"
and for the next eighteen months his mind wavered between
peace or war as the better course for the country.[53] Jefferson
was right in predicting that the mission would be delayed. The
cabinet demanded a three-man commission; and after the two
additional envoys were appointed, obstruction continued for
several months. This was not Adams' doing but, retired to
Quincy, he was very slow to combat it. The success of the war
system, the Hamiltonians realized, depended on the public
conviction of its necessity to defend the nation against France.
To act on the contrary assumption, as Adams appeared to do,
was like declaring "the emperor has no clothes," which, of
course, had been the Republican cry all along. How was it
possible to cripple the Republican party, stamp out sedition,
raise a standing army, consolidate the national government,
and go filibustering in the Spanish dominions when the

rationale for these enterprises was taken away? Adams drew
back as he slowly realized he had been the dupe of political
folly. He grew more and more anxious about the army, and
later said he made peace with France in order to squelch
Hamilton's grandiose schemes of war and conquest.[54] Mounting debt and taxes recalled him to the Whig doctrines learned
in his youth. "All the declarations, as well as the demonstrations, of Trenchard and Gordon, Bolingbroke, Barnard and
Walpole, Hume, Burgh, and Burke, rush upon my memory
and frighten me out of my wits," he confessed.[55] Finally, in
May 1800, he dismissed two of Hamilton's servants in the
cabinet, Pickering and McHenry, irrevocably splitting the
Federalist party.

As the election of 1800 drew near, rumors surfaced of a new
rapprochement between Adams and Jefferson. They had supposedly struck a bargain to make joint stock against the Hamilton party and to trade offices. The cabinet removals, Pickering
charged, were part of the bargain, as was Jefferson's casting
vote in the Senate to confirm the nomination of John Quincy
Adams' father-in-law to a federal office.[56] Adams was said to
speak approvingly of Jefferson once again, to curse Hamilton,
and to inveigh endlessly against the "British faction," the very
existence of which he had earlier denied. The Federalist caucus had voted to give equal support to both the party's nomi-
nees, Adams and Charles Cotesworth Pinckney of South Carolina. Hamilton calculated that Jefferson and Pinckney would
split the South Carolina vote; if so, and if the Federalist margin
of four years ago held up and the party's candidates were
equally supported elsewhere, Pinckney would be elected president. The Pinckneys were different but the plot was the same
as in 1796. In the later stages of the campaign, Hamilton
published a tirade against Adams' character, which, uninten-
tionally, was equally damning of his own. The animosity between the two wings of the party, together with Adams' apparent tacking to the Republican position, gave some substance to

the rumors of a Jefferson-Adams coalition. But, of course, the rumors were untrue. The two men were much too seriously alienated. Politically, 1800 was not 1796. As the Republican party regained strength, Jefferson felt neither the need nor the desire for association with Adams. In fact, he was probably embarrassed by the circulation moderate Federalists gave to his letters of 1796 declaring Adams to be a firm and decided republican.[57] As for Adams, no doubt he considered the Virginian a small evil compared to the Federalist madmen of the "British faction," but his enmity made any idea of a rapprochement absurd.

The election was bitterly contested by both parties. Everyone seemed to understand that the decision would fix the political destiny of the country for decades to come. Around Jefferson, imaged as the democratic "man of the people," the Republicans achieved unprecedented unity of action and feeling. Political parties might still be condemned in theory, but they matured rapidly under the concrete pressure of forming electoral tickets, broadcasting principles and issues, and mobilizing opinion at the country crossroads and in the city wards. Federalists were astounded by the industry and organization of the Republicans, even in New England where, it was said, they were "trooped, officered, regimented" in a manner never equaled by the militia. "Every threshing floor, every husking, every party work on a house-frame or raising a building, the very funerals are infected with bawlers or whisperers against government."[58] Distrusting democracy, "a party of notables" (in Max Weber's terminology), the Federalists were ill-equipped to conduct a campaign in the electorate. The war system, with its engines of terrorizing public opinion, was collapsing around them, while the discord within the party left them dismayed and desperate. The leadership in the Senate pushed legislation to set up a joint committee of the two houses which, meeting in secret session, would have final canvassing authority over the electoral vote. Of course, Federalists would control the committee. But William Duane, the Republican editor in Philadelphia, got hold of the bill while it was still under the wraps of secrecy and published it, thereby ensuring its subsequent defeat in the House as well as his own indictment for a false, scandalous, and malicious libel of the Senate. As early as April, the Republicans scored the first victory—many thought the decisive victory—of the campaign when they swept the election for the New York legislature. In that state, as in several others, the legislature chose the presidential electors. Hamilton at once wrote to the governor, John Jay, urging him to convene the lame-duck Federalist legislature in order to change the electoral law and thus contrive to reverse the Republican verdict. Otherwise, he warned, the country faced "a revolution after the manner of Bonaparte."[59] But there was honor among Federalists: Jay quietly buried the proposal.

Not long after the New York election, Jefferson stopped by the president's office on some official business. "Well, I understand that you are to beat me in this contest," Adams said with a trace of asperity. Jefferson replied that the contest was not between them but between opposing systems of politics. "Its motion is from principle, not from you or myself. Were we both to die today, tomorrow two other names would be put in the place of ours, without any change in the motion of the machinery."[60] Jefferson did not stay to argue the matter, but if he had he might have pointed to whole clusters of Republican principles and doctrines which, in his opinion, made the conflict with the Federalists irrepressible.[61] First, freedom of religion, freedom of speech and press, the right of the people, inseparable from their sovereignty, to criticize and oppose governing authority, and the responsiveness of rulers both to public opinion and to the spirit of science and progress. He had in mind the Sedition Act, obviously, but also the "hue and cry against the sacred name of philosophy" and the concerted Federalist campaign to make religion a political issue by, among other things, conscripting to the pulpit and portraying him as an infidel. Second, the preservation of the Constitution, the separation of powers, and the rights of the states. In his political letters, Jefferson reiterated his long-standing opposition to a system of administration and finance that led to a "monarchical" executive, that multiplied offices, taxes and debt, and sank the states under a consolidated government. "Our country is too large to have its affairs conducted by a single government," he declared. "Public servants at such a distance . . . by rendering detection impossible to their constituents, will invite the public agents to corruption, plunder, and waste. . . . The true theory of our Constitution is surely the wisest and best, that the states are independent as to everything within themselves, and united as to everything respecting foreign nations." Third, "free commerce with all nations, political connection with none." The principle of divorce and disentanglement from Europe was shared by Adams, but the Federalist system, as he discovered too late, turned upon British trade and power. Foreign influence in American politics was an old story. Jefferson and his party had earlier formed such strong attachments to the French Revolution that they were vulnerable to the charge of subservience to France. But these attachments were now dead, like the Revolution, Jefferson insisted. His own hopes for the Revolution had been jolted over the years, yet as late as 1798 he had kept faith with the French republic. Finally, the 18th Brumaire of Napoleon Bonaparte, overthrowing the republic and establishing a dictatorial consulate, crushed Jefferson's last hopes. He had looked upon France as a commercial ally, but her atrocities on American commerce had produced a crisis that threatened to destroy the country's liberties. He had looked upon France as the spearhead of republicanism in Europe, but the people's longings for liberty had been harnessed to Napoleon's imperial ambitions. He had thought the success of the French republic necessary to secure the American. Nothing was left of that theory in 1800. Jefferson was resigned, at last, to an American destiny in a world of its own. "It is very material," he wrote to a Republican leader, "for the [people] to be made sensible that their own character and situation are materially different from the French, and that whatever may be the fate of republicanism there, we are able to preserve it inviolate here."[62] Partiality to France was no longer justified; neutrality was no longer enough; divorce from Europe was the true policy, though it would be more easily asserted than accomplished. Adams, had he heard these sentiments, might have chuckled. Jefferson had recovered from his delusions about the French Revolution! And whatever Jefferson might think of him, he had Adams to thank for ending the old alliance, saving the peace, and opening the way to withdrawal from Europe.

The government was settling into the new capital on the Potomac, a Jeffersonian seat despised by Adams and most Federalists, when the election of 1800 drew to a close. The Republican margin in the electoral vote, 73 to 65, failed to reflect the margin of the party's victory at the polls. But the victory was jeopardized by a treacherous abyss in the electoral system. Under the Constitution, prior to the Twelfth Amendment, separate ballots were not required for president and vice-president. Electors voted for two candidates, the second office going to the runner-up. Jefferson and his running-mate, Aaron Burr, received an equal number of electoral votes, which threw the choice into the House of Representatives. "Seventy-three for Mr. Jefferson and seventy-three for Mr. Burr," Adams brooded. "May the peace and welfare of the country be promoted by this result!"[63] In the House, the lame-duck Federalist majority, elected in the year of terror, plotted to annul the popular verdict either by creating an interregnum or by dealing Burr into the presidency. Embittered by defeat, Adams stood aloof from the contest, seemingly indifferent to its outcome or to its dangers. Between two ambitious demagogues there was perhaps not much to choose, but he considered Jefferson a lesser evil than the cunning upstart,

Burr. In this he agreed with Hamilton, though he did nothing
to aid Jefferson. One Federalist plan called for Congress to set
aside the election and name the president *pro tem* of the Senate
or some other officer the chief executive. Alarmed by this,
Jefferson summoned up his courage to call on the president.
The plan was fraught with "incalculable consequences," he
told Adams, which executive action might prevent. But Adams
apparently saw nothing wrong with the plan, and observed
that Jefferson himself could end the crisis instantly by making
certain pledges to the Federalists, pledges he consistently refused. For the first time in their long association, as Jefferson
recalled the interview, he and Adams parted with genuine
personal displeasure.[64] It was their last parting. Finally, February 17, on the thirty-sixth ballot, Jefferson was elected president. Winding up its affairs in a fury of activity, the Adams
administration appointed hardened Federalists to a host of
judgeships and other offices—an act of "personal unkindness"
Jefferson would find difficult to forgive. Early on the morning
of March 4, hours before the inauguration of his successor,
Adams fled the city, returning to the obscurity of the Massachusetts home he had called "Peace Field" but now renamed
"Stony Field."

  Jefferson's inaugural address was both an epilogue to a long
political drama and a prologue to things to come. It was a lofty
summation of the Republican creed, elevated to a creed of
Americanism. Jefferson traced its principles back to the
American Revolution, thereby authenticating it for the national consciousness, and he pledged to make this creed the
touchstone of American government. The address made a
bold bid for the restoration of harmony and affection. "We
have called by different names brethren of the same principle.
We are all republicans: we are all federalists." Believing that
the mass of Americans, omitting the extreme Federalists, were
fundamentally united in their political sentiments, Jefferson
saw no excuse for the strife, hatred, and fanaticism—the insig-

nia of European politics—that had rocked the republic in
recent years. He looked to the gradual disappearance of parties and "a perfect consolidation of political sentiments" as
government was restored to true principles, as individuals
were left to their own devices, and as the nation realized its
destiny in a "chosen country" apart from the Old World. Finally, and above all, the first inaugural was a commitment to
ongoing political change through the democratic process of
open debate, popular participation, and free elections. Jefferson named "absolute acquiescence in the decisions of the
majority, the vital principle of republics, from which there is no
appeal but to force." This principle, to be effective, demanded
unmolested freedom of opinion and debate. "If there be any
among us," he said, alluding to the delusions of '98, "who
would wish to dissolve this Union or to change its republican
form, let them stand undisturbed as monuments of the safety
with which error of opinion may be tolerated where reason is
left free to combat it." Federalist leaders had reckoned the
strength of government on Old World standards: army and
navy, the patronage of "the rich, the well born, and the able,"
great treasury, ministerial mastery, central command, the
panoply of office and the splendor of state. But Jefferson called
the American government, for all its feebleness by these standards, "the strongest government on earth" because it was the
only one founded on the affections, the opinions, and the
suffrages of the people.[65]

Jefferson later said that "the revolution of 1800 . . . was as
real a revolution in the principles of our government as that of
1776 was in its form; not effected indeed by the sword, as that,
but by the rational and peaceable instrument of reform, the
suffrage of the people."[66] The Constitution became an instrument of democracy, change became possible without violence
or destruction, and the process began by which the government could go forward with the continuing consent of the

governed. If the frame was that of 1776, the picture was different, for a number of reasons, but in considerable part because of the transforming influence of the French Revolution. It had revived that "spirit of revolution" in the people without which, in Jefferson's philosophy, free government slid into corruption and tyranny. It had communicated its own egalitarian passion to American politics, exalted the popular will over constituted authority, revitalized an old Whig ideology against privilege and repression, and given sharp definition to competing political ideals previously vague or inchoate. The development of political parties, which no one had wanted, came largely in response to forces released by the French Revolution; and the party of Jefferson, by assimilating elements of that revolution to the creed of the American Revolution, secured the democratic line of advance. It was the second revolution that made the first a datum of American *democratic* consciousness; but it was the third revolution, "the revolution of 1800," that warranted no further revolution would be necessary. Democracy superseded revolution.

Jefferson understood this change, indeed he personified it; but its true significance was lost on John Adams. Coddling his disappointments at Quincy, the only revolution he could see was that of crafty politicians bilking the people. While the Federalists had attempted to save the people from their own worst enemy, themselves, the Republicans established their ascendancy by pandering to popular vices and illusions. Democratic politics was simply a Richardsonian plot of pursuit, seduction, and disaster. "Democracy is Lovelace, and the people are Clarissa. The artful villain will pursue the innocent young girl to her ruin and her death."[67] Adams continued to view Jefferson as a creature of party, a Gallomaniac, and a demagogue. The more he reflected on his own downfall, however, the more he concluded that the Federalists were no better, perhaps were worse, than the Republicans. The two parties fed upon each other's filth, like a famous species of hogs: "Hogs of Westphalia are a saving brood, / What one lets drop, the other takes as food."[68] Such was the character of parties. The vice was entailed on the nation because men like Jefferson, deceived by the French Revolution, had taught the people to think of their government as a democracy rather than a balanced republic after Adams' vision.

FOUR

Retrospect and Prospect

IT WAS SCARCELY TO BE EXPECTED THAT THE VICTOR AND THE
vanquished in the "revolution of 1800" would ever be reunited
in friendship. Remarkably, they were, though only after the
passage of eleven years. Adams withdrew into his shell at
Quincy. His influence gone and only his books and his plow
between him and the grave, he seemed sullenly resigned to his
fate; but defeat struck at his pride, and he soon began rum-
maging over the past to discover its cause. Recalling his entire
career, he wondered if it was not an almost classic case of the
ingratitude of republics toward their leaders. "I always consider the whole nation as my children," he said, "but they have
almost all been undutiful to me." That all his efforts to serve
and instruct the nation would be met with persecution, injustice, and ingratitude had been prophesied to him by an ambas-
sador at the court of Versailles in 1784. The prophesy had
been "completely fulfilled," as Adams always knew it would
be.[1] He found solace in the life of Cicero, who had also borne
the slings and arrows of all parties. Conscious of his own purity
and integrity, Cicero, in his defense, had been driven to assertions that many thought proof of vanity but which Adams took
as proof of the envy and dishonor of little men. "Pushed and
injured and provoked as I am, I blush not to imitate the
Roman," he said. The old charge of vanity had no terrors for
him. "Every persecuted man, persecuted because he is envied,
must be an egotist or a hypocrite." And besides, as he would
philosophize to a young friend, "Vanity is the cordial drop
which makes the bitter cup of life go down."[2]

Gradually, as his spirits revived, Adams spoke out boldly in defense of his public career. In 1807 he engaged in an epistolary tirade against Mercy Warren, once a dear friend, for her *History of the American Revolution*. Mrs. Warren slighted his revolutionary services, made him a figure of passion and prejudice, and accused him of apostacy from republican principles. Adams, in turn, accused her of writing history in order to gratify the feelings of the Republican party. He was boastful of his own services, believing they exceeded those of any of his contemporaries, and insisted he was, as he had always been, a better republican than Jefferson. Much of this was mean and petty as well as vain. Mrs. Warren at first attempted to reason with him, but finally dismissed Adams' performance as "the ravings of a maniac."[3] The pommeling of Mrs. Warren, and through her of all the Republican assailants of his reputation, was only a prelude to Adams' denunciation of the Federalist party in a prolonged series of letters published in the Boston *Patriot*. Principally a vindication of his presidency, the letters attacked Hamilton, Pickering, and the "British party" who, Adams charged, had silently conspired with the Republicans to accomplish his downfall. As he later summed up the analysis, "The [Federalist] party committed suicide; they killed themselves and the national President (not their President) at one shot, and then, as foolishly or maliciously, indicted me for the murder."[4] The main count in the indictment, the second mission to France, was actually "the most splendid diamond in my crown," Adams said. It was a disinterested act—between self-serving partisans left and right, the only American act. The more he pondered the subject, the more he made the peace with France the virtuous symbol of his entire career. Thus he could write in 1815 that he wanted no other inscription on his tombstone than this: "Here lies John Adams, who took upon himself the responsibility of the peace with France in the year 1800."[5] He sometimes said he was careless of fame, but this, too, was a piece of vanity. A passionate commitment to his fame caused him to cast off the mantle of oblivion he had wrapped around himself in 1801 and can alone explain the personal preoccupation of many years to vindicate his place in history, often at the expense of eminent contemporaries.

Renewal of the old friendship with Jefferson was no part of this scenario. In his heart Adams may have wished it, for he still liked Jefferson, and such was the strength of his feelings that once he had contracted a friendship he could never lose it all. But only victors enjoy the luxury of magnanimity. The first move would have to come from Jefferson, who made it, in a roundabout way, in 1804. Mrs. Adams had written to him a letter of condolence on the death of his younger daughter. Jefferson thought he saw in the letter proof that their friendship, at least, was unbroken, and he seized on the opening to invite a reconciliation with the former president. Reviewing the ancient friendship, Jefferson observed that for his part only one act of Adams' life, the so-called "midnight appointments," had ever given him a moment's personal displeasure. "They were from among my most ardent political enemies, from whom no faithful cooperation could ever be expected, and laid me under the embarrassment of acting through men whose views were to defeat mine; or to encounter the odium of putting others in their places. It seemed but common justice to leave a successor free to act by instruments of his own choice." (Jefferson removed a number of the eleventh-hour appointees, and was particularly irritated by the new federal judgeships, their tenure running for life, created by the Federalist Judiciary Act of 1801. The act, with the judgeships, was repealed by the Republicans in 1802.) This, Jefferson confessed, "left something for friendship to forgive," and after a time he had forgiven it, cordially and completely.[6]

Jefferson expected that Mrs. Adams would share his letter with her husband. She did not, but undertook to speak for him in reply. In filling federal offices, Adams had simply exercised the duty imposed on him by the Constitution. Government could not be suspended in the interval between one president and the next. No act of personal unkindness was intended. But as long as Jefferson was airing grievances, she would disclose those actions of his that had finally severed the bonds of friendship. Jefferson's election had been effected by "the blackest calumny" against the incumbent. The chief of the calumniators was James T. Callender, who had been tried, convicted, fined and imprisoned for violation of the Sedition Act. One of Jefferson's first executive acts was to liberate this wretch and remit his fine, after which Callender, turning on his former benefactor, revealed that he had been a paid hireling of the vice-president. "This," Mrs. Adams declared, "was the sword that cut asunder the Gordian knot, which could not be untied by all the efforts of party spirit, by rivalship, by jealousy or any other malignant fiend." [7] She went on to allude to another act of unkindness which Jefferson's own reflection would readily enough suggest. When it did not, she reminded him of his removal of her son John Quincy from the office of commissioner of bankruptcy in Massachusetts. Jefferson was able to explain this incident to her entire satisfaction. (Under the former law, appointment to the occasional office of commissioner had been by a federal judge; when the law was changed to give the appointment to the president, Jefferson had no knowledge the younger Adams had ever served in the office.) As to Callender, he said that the small payments made to him were mere charities, "no more meant as encouragements to his scurrilities than those I give to a beggar at my door are meant as rewards for the vices of his life." [8] This was less than candid, for Jefferson's "charities" were so intimately blended with the production of partisan tracts he acknowledged to be scurrilous as to require an act of naïveté to separate them. Mrs. Adams did not believe him. Jefferson was on firmer ground in restating his position that regardless of the atrocities perpetrated by the press, whether against him or against Adams, the federal government had no authority to suppress opinion. He had, accordingly, upon becoming president considered the Sedition Act "a nullity" and freed all its victims. Mrs. Adams, whose polemical skills fully equalled Jefferson's, replied with a discourse on the blindness and licentiousness of party spirit which threatened the. survival of the republic. She defended the constitutionality of the Sedition Act and said that even if it were unconstitutional, the judiciary, not the executive, should declare it. Jefferson countered with his own theory of tripartite balance founded on the separation of powers. Each of the three branches of the government had a right to decide questions of constitutionality for itself; if the judiciary alone possessed that right, it would tyrannize over the others. Mrs. Adams had no wish to argue such questions. A correspondence that had begun with her expression of heartfelt sympathy over the death of a daughter had turned into a confrontation of political principles. She returned to the major personal grievance centering on Callender. "It was not until after the circumstances concurred to place you in the light of a rewarder and encourager of a libeler, whom you could not but detest and despise, that I withdrew the esteem I had long entertained for you." [9] Mrs. Adams would not forgive, and on this note she declared the correspondence closed.

The correspondence of several months was carried on without John Adams' knowledge or suspicion. When Mrs. Adams later showed it to him, he had nothing to say. Although her political opinions were to the right of his, and she was the more fiery politician, there is no reason to believe that the outcome would have been different had he participated in the correspondence. He was still licking his wounds in 1804, and his wife apparently wished to save him the pain of reopening them. He wrote few letters and generally avoided political questions; but the evidence suggests that, for all his ineradicable affection, he felt no more forgiving of Jefferson than his wife and thought little better of him as a philosopher and a statesman than the New England Federalist leaders. He was a man under French

influence; his scientific speculations were but "pitiful baga-
telles"; he despised the wholesome sentiments of the Christian
religion. His patronage of Callender and a host of Republican
libelers was not only a blot on his moral character but proof he
was a captive of party.[10] The course of Jefferson's administration confirmed Adams' fears for it. He condemned the repeal
of the Judiciary Act, partisan removals from office, repeal of
the internal taxes, and cutbacks of American naval power. The
only important Jeffersonian measure he approved was the
Louisiana Purchase.[11] As he saw it, the nation was suffering
from a distemper, democracy, "and when it is once set in
motion and obtains a majority, it converts everything good,
bad, and indifferent into the dominant epidemic."[12] It had
invaded Massachusetts and to all intents and purposes con-
verted Adams' balanced constitution into a simple democracy.
Jefferson was wholly consumed by this epidemic. "I wish him
no ill," Adams wrote in 1804. "I envy him not. I shudder at the
calamities, which I fear his conduct is preparing for his country
from a mean thirst of popularity, an inordinate ambition, and a
want of sincerity."[13] Jefferson, of course, supposed that a free
government grew strong not by combatting the popular will
but by sympathizing with it and nudging it into constructive
channels. As he stated the issue between the parties to Mrs.
Adams: "One fears most the ignorance of the people; the other
the selfishness of rulers independent of them."[14] The idea that
democracy traveled a circular route, through licentiousness,
demagoguery, and egalitarian delusion, back to despotism—
an idea rooted in political philosophy including Adams'
own—was alien to Jefferson's outlook.

The first essay at reconciliation failed, but a second seven
years later succeeded. Why? Nothing was more important in
preparing the way than a change in Adams' political posture.
His articles in the Boston *Patriot*, commenced in 1807, made
him *persona non grata* to New England Federalists. They were a
necessary purgative for his return to political health, and in

effect, if not in name, he became a Republican. The purging coincided with the foreign crisis of Jefferson's second administration. The War of the Third Coalition rocked the Atlantic world; relations between the United States and Great Britain rapidly deteriorated on issues of neutral rights and impressment of American seamen. The two nations were brought to the brink of war in June 1807 when the British ship *Leopard* brutally attacked the American frigate *Chesapeake* off the coast of Virginia. Adams rallied to the Jefferson administration. In this he followed the course of his son John Quincy Adams, now a United States senator from Massachusetts. John Quincy, though a Federalist, had his father's penchant for independence, and in the reciprocity of influence between the two men he now held the upper hand. War was averted over the *Chesapeake* Affair, but the crisis worsened until in December Jefferson proposed the embargo of American ships, seamen, and productions from the high seas. The Massachusetts senator enthusiastically endorsed the embargo. John Adams also approved of it, as an alternative to war, though he inclined to think it "cowardly" and never entered into the Jeffersonian theory of "peaceable coercion," the theory of forcing justice on foreign nations by withholding American commerce, which the measure assumed.[15] John Quincy attended the Republican caucus in Congress in January 1808. He was then repudiated by the Federalist-controlled legislature of Massachusetts and forced to resign. Before leaving Washington he called on the president, who had known and admired the younger Adams since his seventeenth year when they had promenaded in Paris together, and disclosed a disunionist plot among bitter-end Federalists in New England. He was later charged with selling out to the Republicans to save his political career. While the charge lacked merit, it was not without some semblance of truth, for in 1809 Adams' Republican career was launched by his appointment as United States minister to the court of St. Petersburg. Naturally enough, the father was suspected of going over to the Republicans and, in due time, making up with Jefferson for the sake of his son.

The evidence of Adams' changing politics was not only to be found in national affairs, however. In 1810 his old friend—Jefferson's too—Elbridge Gerry became the second Republican governor of Massachusetts. Adams vigorously supported him. As the second war with Britain came on, and Gerry attempted to range Massachusetts behind the Madison administration, he purged the Federalists from office, castigated their leaders as tories, traitors, and disunionists, and denounced the pulpit politics of the clergy. Adams rejoiced. Yet he denied that he had changed his politics. "The charge of 'change of politics' . . . deserves no other answer than this, 'The Hyperfederalists are become Jacobins, and the Hyperrepublicans are become Federalists. John Adams remains *semper idem*, both Federalist and Republican in every rational and intelligible sense of both these words.' "[16] In fact, he had changed, though the motion was only that of a balance wheel. He had always conceived of his political role as an antagonist of extremes, shifting his weight to the right or left depending on his sense of where the greater danger lay, but never altering his fundamental principles. Thus in 1770, thinking American libertarians needed a lesson in the supremacy of the laws, he had defended Captain Preston and the British soldiers charged with the Boston Massacre; at the time of the treaty of peace, he had attempted to neutralize French power by bidding for British friendship; after Shays' Rebellion, fearing rampant democracy, he had drawn attention to the virtues of monarchy and aristocracy in a balanced constitution; and so on. Now, in the prolonged crisis leading to the War of 1812, the danger came from the political right, particularly from New England Federalists who had sold their souls to Britain for partisan and commercial gain. With an eye cocked to his son's political fortunes, but with the national interest uppermost in mind, Adams threw his weight into the Republican scale.

After Jefferson's retirement to Monticello in 1809, America's most eminent physician, Dr. Benjamin Rush of Philadelphia, took upon himself the task of reuniting his old friends. In them the spirit of the American Revolution was personified, Rush thought, and their continued estrangement was a national calamity. He suggested as much to Adams but got only a cryptic response. Later he broached the subject to Jefferson, who forwarded his correspondence of 1804 with Mrs. Adams and asked Rush to judge for himself whether it admitted a revival of friendly intercourse.[17] In 1811, Edward Coles, President Madison's private secretary, made a social call on Adams. He reminisced freely about American politics and voiced old grievances against Jefferson, especially as connected with the election of 1800. Coles, a young Albemarle friend of Jefferson's, suggested that these matters might be viewed in a different light. And when he assured Adams of Jefferson's continued affection, the old man burst out, "I always loved Jefferson, and still love him."[18] The report soon reached Monticello. "This is enough for me," Jefferson declared to Rush. "And now, my friend, my dear friend," the doctor at once wrote to Adams, "permit me again to suggest to you to receive the olive branch which has thus been offered to you by the hand of a man who still loves you. Fellow laborers in erecting the great fabric of American independence! . . . Embrace—embrace each other!"[19] Adams replied in a vein more comic than serious. His past differences with Jefferson (and Rush too) were "all miserable frivolities." He preferred formal speeches to Congress, Jefferson written messages. He favored formal weekly levees; "Jefferson's whole eight years was a levee." "Jefferson and Rush were for liberty and straight hair. I thought curled hair was as republican as straight." Rush solemnly exhorted Adams to forgive his enemies, as if he had ever considered Jefferson an enemy. "This is not so; I have always loved him as a friend. If I ever received or suspected any injury from him, I have forgotten it long and long ago." But why did

Rush make such a fuss over these two old warriors, Adams and
Jefferson, exchanging letters? "I have nothing to say to him,
but to wish him an easy journey to heaven, when he goes. . . .
And he can have nothing to say to me, but to bid me to make
haste and be ready. Time and chance, however, or possibly
design," Adams added jauntily, "may produce ere long a letter
between us."[20] Within a week, on January 1, 1812, he opened
the correspondence with greetings on the new year and the
promise of "two pieces of homespun" produced in his quarter
of the Union. Jefferson, caught off guard by Adams' humor,
promptly responded with an essay on domestic manufactures,
only the next day to discover that the "homespun" consisted of
two volumes of *Lectures on Rhetoric and Oratory* by John Quincy
Adams.[21]

The correspondence continued without interruption for
fourteen years, until they were both ready to die. A marvelous
vindication of the spirit of friendship over the spirit of party, it
also carried symbolic meaning for the nation at large. Adams
and Jefferson were well aware of this. As their revolutionary
comrades fell away one by one, they became the last of the
founders, the great patriarchs of the nation's heritage, and it
almost seemed that renewal of the ancient friendship was the
highest service they might yet render their country. The correspondence was not a patriotic exercise, however. It was an
expression on the late landscape of the philosophical genius
that had guided the early footsteps of the republic. It testified
to, and in time became a testament of, the intellectual spa-
ciousness that distinguished the founders' generation and
would not be seen in American statesmanship again. For
Adams and Jefferson the American Revolution was a philosophical adventure no less than a political one. All history, all
learning, all mankind were concerned in it, and while they
often read the directives differently, neither man could any
more separate his politics from a humanistic frame of values
than he could see the other as an enemy to the holy cause of

liberty. The correspondence, both a retrospect on the founding and a somewhat anxious prospect on the new age, evòked qualities of mind and heart that may have been ultimately more significant, because they were shared, than all the continuing clashes of opinion and temperament between the aged patriots.

Their letters traversed an immense intellectual terrain: the philosophy of Plato, the pronunciation of ancient Greek, Indian origins and antiquities, neology, spiritualism and materialism, the uses and abuses of grief, the nature of aristocracy, the French Revolution, the character of Bonaparte, and so on. Adams turned 77 in 1812, and Jefferson 69, but they addressed questions of the past, present, and future with a nimbleness younger men might envy. Both enjoyed good health for their years, the adoration of children and grandchildren, and the veneration of their countrymen. Reading was their favorite pastime, and mixed with ample writing, especially in Jefferson's case, it kept their minds alert. While both men welcomed the renewal of correspondence, Adams entered into it with an eagerness Jefferson never felt. He wrote at least four letters to Jefferson's one, despite the palsy— "quiveration," he called it—in his hands which made writing difficult. It was Adams who generally introduced the subjects for discussion and thus directed the course of the correspondence. Jefferson could not keep up with him. He was a much busier man than his Massachusetts friend. Not only was there the management of a large estate with all its farms, and then, during the last decade of his life, the work of founding the University of Virginia, but he was literally deluged with correspondence. This, he said, was "the burden of my life." In a single year he received 1,267 letters. They were letters of inquiry, for the most part, seeking his aid or advice on some project or theory, usually from perfect strangers, but always written civilly, therefore deserving civil answers. Moreover, a letter for Jefferson tended to become a disquisition. The result was that he was chained to his writing table several hours of every day. "Is this life?" he finally wrote rebelliously to Adams. "At best it is but the life of a mill-horse, who sees no end to his circle but in death." [22] Adams was not "persecuted" in this way. He was not popular. He had little of Jefferson's Delphic reputation as a sage. And, as he confessed, Adams employed two expedients to discourage correspondents: returning no answer at all or giving "gruff, short, unintelligible, mysterious, enigmatical, or pedantical answers." Jefferson's nature, concededly, placed these methods out of his power. [23] The correspondence proved a godsend to Adams. With little to do but read and poke about his farm, he made it his "refuge against ennui," spilling out ideas and reflections in an epistolary assault that stunned Jefferson. [24] Being constantly in arrears was bad enough but, contemplating the forest of Adams' topics, he sometimes felt like Theocritus' woodcutter on Mount Ida gazing at the thousands of trees and asking himself, "What first shall I gather?" [25] Coolly, he set his sights on a single one and let the rest go.

The contrast between Adams' random loquacity and Jefferson's studiously composed responses characterized the correspondence as a whole. Adams wrote as he talked. Sprightly, pungent, spontaneous, running off in half a dozen directions at once, his letters gained in naturalness what they lost in logical development of ideas. Jefferson's were more artful, coherent, felicitous, tending to be rounded essays on some topic of learning or experience. Adams was bold, even reckless, in expression of opinion, Jefferson deliberate and reserved. Adams was full of himself, turning everything around his own thoughts and feelings; Jefferson was less egocentric, more detached, more interested in general truths disclosed by inquiry than in psychological truths disclosed to oneself. Jefferson was grave, never descending to notice his friend's teases and jests. The world sometimes seemed to Adams a bedlam, to be understood only in riddles; and shocking, laughing, and scolding were his delights. He liked to speculate on politics and religion, where Jefferson followed him easily enough—indeed, Adams remarked, any speculation dispatched to Monticello was like sending coal to Newcastle—though his preferred realm was the sciences, where Adams rarely ventured. History afforded many topics of discussion, but for Adams history was not only a branch of humane learning but a critical post of observation on the present. Mention of anything was likely to lead him into historical discourse; dwelling on his own past was almost an obsession. Jefferson, on the other hand, felt an aversion to looking back. He did not enjoy staring into the shadows of his own reflection and, as he said, preferred the dreams of the future to the history of the past. While he was no less sensitive than Adams to his title to fame, he was much more philosophical about it, easily resigning himself to the judgment of posterity. Perhaps he could afford to be. Adams' fame was less secure. He still had old scores to settle (with Paine, Franklin, Hamilton, and others) and he did not hesitate to throw the vexing question to Monticello, "How many gauntlets am I destined to run? How many martyrdoms must I suffer?"[26]

The books that they read, and the way they read them, offers another index to the contrasting styles of the two men. Adams was a voracious reader, even after his sight failed and he had to find other eyes to read for him. He read and reread ancient classics; read the complete works of Lord Bolingbroke (of whom Burke had asked the devastating question, "Who now reads Bolingbroke? Who ever read him through?") for, he said, at least the fifth time; swallowed fifteen volumes of Baron Grimm's memoirs in one gulp, along with twelve volumes of Dupuis on religious imposture; read Jesuitical history, Scott's romances, and early New England chronicles. Jefferson was astounded by one annual report: "Forty-three volumes read in one year, and 12 of them quartos! Dear Sir, how I envy you! Half a dozen octavos in that space of time is as much as I am allowed."[27] Jefferson's reading, if much less in quantity, was much more discriminating. The ancient writers, with whom he sought to beguile the weariness of old age, had a stronger hold on him than on Adams; and to the classics he added liberal doses of mathematics and science. Adams was a combative reader, as is evidenced by the marginalia in his books, as well as by the enjoyment he got from reading what he hated, while Jefferson, who rarely left more than his initials in a book, was an absorptive one. The former was more adventuresome during these declining years; the latter generally stuck to what he knew, living on the literary capital accumulated over several score of years.

It was a more or less silent premise of the correspondence that politics would be adjourned. Jefferson underscored the point in his first letter. He had taken final leave of politics. "I think little of them, and say less. I have given up newspapers in exchange for Tacitus and Thucydides, for Newton and Euclid; and I find myself much the happier."[28] Adams, too, professed to be "weary of politics," yet he could not dismiss it, and he peppered the correspondence with controversial matters Jefferson was reluctant to touch. The friendship was resumed on the eve of the War of 1812. Both men fervently supported the war. Jefferson had hoped to win the second contest with Britain by peaceful means, by economic coercion, but "the lions and tigers of Europe" demanded American blood, and so the war came as a mournful necessity from which, nevertheless, he anticipated a new epoch of American liberty and nationality. It was his hope, as he told Adams, that the war would end in "indemnity for the past, security for the future, and complete emancipation from Anglomany, Gallomany, and all the manias of demoralized Europe."[29] This was all very well—it was Adams' hope too—but the New Englander could not refrain from criticizing Jefferson and Madison for policies that, in his opinion, had invited war with Britain and left the country virtually defenseless as well as disunited when it came. The Virginians' hostility to the navy was his principal complaint.

Because of it the commerce of New England was sacrificed and popularity played into the hands of disorganizing Federalists, whose policy was war with France, alliance with Britain, dependence on British naval power and British manufactures, and, in the ultimate extremity, separation from the Union. Adams condemned these madmen, of course, but lamented the policies that had given too much apology for them. Without a navy, he declared, the Union must be "a brittle China vase." [30] Increasingly, in Adams' thought, the idea of the Union tended to replace the idea of constitutional balance as the rock of political salvation. As the war progressed, the navy was built. Adams took pride and found vindication in its gallant victories. At times in the past Jefferson had exceeded him in the advocacy of naval power, but Adams had been "the early and constant advocate of wooden walls," as Jefferson acknowledged, and if while president he had differed with him, the difference was one of priorities and timing, not of principle. [31] To most of Adams' criticism Jefferson was silent or evasive. He did not wish to argue questions likely to give offence, and where necessary he went out of his way to soften asperities Adams still felt.

The reconciliation was only a year and a half old when Adams called Jefferson to account for portraying him as a kind of vandal against science and progress in a letter to Joseph Priestley in March 1801. This letter and another to Priestley on religion had turned up in a book concerned with the rise of Unitarianism, *Memoirs of the Late Reverend Theophilus Lindsey*, published in London in 1812 and put into Adams' hands. He saw at once that the work was destined to "produce a noise" in the United States, especially in his quarter, for it contained the letters of many American Unitarians, including ministers in Congregational pulpits in New England. But it was Jefferson's political letter that at once agitated Adams. In it Jefferson had taken his first opportunity as president of the United States to welcome his friend, the English refugee scientist and theologian, to the country, and to assure him that he would not again be threatened by bigotry and persecution masquerading under the form of law, such as "that libel on legislation," the Alien Law. "What an effort, my dear Sir, of bigotry in politics and religion have we gone through! The barbarians really flattered themselves they should be able to bring back the time of Vandalism. . . . We were to look backwards, not forwards, for improvement; the President himself declaring in one of his answers to addresses, that we were never to expect to go beyond [our ancestors] in real science." [32] This last sentence became Adams' theme in an avalanche of letters. He totally disclaimed the sentiments Jefferson had ascribed to him and demanded proof. [33]

Jefferson was shocked that the confidence of his private letters to a friend should be so grossly abused by publication in the memoirs of a man whose name he scarcely knew and at the hands of an author, Thomas Belsham, he had never heard of. (It was neither the first nor the last time he would suffer this grief, and Adams knew enough of it to sympathize with him.) He was actually more anxious about the second letter, on religion, which would again arouse the priesthood against him. As to the political letter, it accurately portrayed the sensations excited in Republican minds by "the terrorism of the day." Adams would find the wanted proof of the charge of ancestor worship in his answer to the Young Men of Philadelphia, May 7, 1798. It did not look personally toward him, however. "You happen to be quoted," Jefferson said, "because you happened to express, more pithily than had been done by themselves, one of the mottoes of the [Federalist] party." He was as far from considering the expression as Adams' deliberate opinion as he was from blaming him, rather than the crew around him, for the persecuting measures of his administration. "You would do me great injustice therefore taking to yourself what was intended for men who were then your secret, as they are now your open enemies." And he closed with the wish that the passions of a former day not be rekindled either between themselves or in public.[34] Adams, contrary to Jefferson's impression, had no intention of going to the newspapers, but he was not mollified by Jefferson's explanation. The ancestral principles praised in his address were those of Christianity and of English and American liberty, and nothing he had said could be fairly construed as expressing hostility to science and improvement.[35] In literal truth, he may have been right, though Jefferson was clearly right as to the spirit of the address. At any rate, as Adams went on to expatiate on "the terrorism of the day" in a way that justified the actions of the government, Jefferson made no further response other than again to urge upon his friend the wisdom of burying the past and resigning himself to the verdict of posterity. Because neither man would risk jeopardizing the reconciliation, it easily survived this little crisis.

"You and I ought not to die, before we have explained ourselves to each other," Adams wrote in July 1813.[36] This seemed more important to him than it did to Jefferson, and in the area that concerned Adams most, political philosophy, it cannot be said that they succeeded. About many things they agreed, from the metaphysical nonsense of Plato to the despotism of Napoleon. Serious issues still divided them, however, issues which Jefferson recognized more clearly than Adams but which, in his view, being rooted in nature were unworthy of dispute between old men with one foot in the grave. The same political parties that agitated the United States had existed through all time. "Whether the power of the people, or that of the αριστοι [aristoi] should prevail, were questions which kept the states of Greece and Rome in eternal convulsions, as they now schizmatize every people whose minds and mouths are not shut up by the gag of a despot. And in fact the terms whig and tory belong to natural, as well as to civil history. They denote the temper and constitution of mind of different individuals." Adams, according to his temperament and circumstances, had sided with the party of the few, Jefferson, from the same cause, with the party of the many. In this there was room neither for priaise nor for blame. Both parties were equally honest. "The next generation will judge, favorably or unfavorably, according to the complexion of individual minds, and the side they shall themselves have taken; [but] . . . nothing new can be added by you or me to what has been said by others, and will be said in every age, in support of conflicting opinions on government." [37]

Quite aside from the fact that the theory failed to explain why he, a Virginia aristocrat and slaveholder, became the partisan of democracy, while Adams, the Yankee commoner, became the partisan of aristocracy, this was a surprising statement from Jefferson, perhaps not to be understood apart from his effort to persuade Adams to draw the mantle of oblivion over the past. He had always had difficulty developing a satisfactory theory of political parties. The notion of the natural duality of political life had appeared in his thought before, but usually combined with exigent social, economic, and ideological factors; and for him to assert that the division of Federalist and Republican was no more than the division between Claudii and Grachii, that no advance had been or could be made in resolving the conflict, seemed to place him in Adams' corner. Adams thought so at once. The eternal battle of aristocrats and democrats: was this not the theme of his *Defence of the Constitutions*, and had he not there remarked on the failure of political science to advance over thousands of years? He went on to confound Jefferson's theory with his own. The theory of the permanence of aristocratic and democratic orders, based on natural inequality, was the same as the theory holding that men are Whig or Tory by nature. "Inequalities of mind and body," Adams wrote, "are so established by God Almighty in his constitution of human nature that no art or policy can ever plane them down to a level." [38] Once tuned in to the old theme, Adams could not give it up. He reviewed the *Defence* and the

Discourses on Davila, complaining that he had been scandalized for them, though their truths could never be refuted. The French Revolution turned into a holocaust for failure to recognize these truths. Aristocracy was a fixture of the universe, its principal pillars being birth and wealth, and every government must make provision both to employ and to control it.

For several months Jefferson took no notice of Adams' rambling reflections on aristocracy. He willingly conceded that Adams had been misunderstood—who among the founders had not been?—at least on the point of wanting to introduce hereditary monarchy and aristocracy in America; but he wished his friend would abandon these old discussions, "equally useless and irksome," and follow him into that Epicurean philosophy, "ease of body and tranquility of mind," which was the *summum bonum* of his remaining days. Finally, however, lest the dialogue lapse into a monologue, Jefferson wielded his axe on one of the trees in Adams' forest of opinions. In Adams' conception, aristocracy was a unit block. Jefferson split the block, distinguishing between *natural* and *artificial* aristocracies. The grounds of the former are virtue and talents, of the latter birth and wealth, and one is valuable while the other is pernicious. "The natural aristocracy," Jefferson wrote, "I consider as the most precious gift of nature for the instruction, the trusts, and government of society. . . . May we not even say that that form of government is the best which provides the most effectually for a pure selection of these natural aristoi into the offices of government? The artificial aristocracy is a mischievous ingredient in government, and provision should be made to prevent its ascendancy." How was this to be accomplished? Adams would lock the "pseudo-aristoi" into a separate chamber of the legislature. But this only armed them for mischief, without any compensatory benefits. It was an unjust intrusion on the popular will; nor was it necessary to protect property from numbers, as often alleged, since property easily found means to protect itself and American experience exploded old fears of the many plundering the few. The natural aristocracy was so fluctuating and fortuitous that it could not be identified or categorized, much less constituted, as an element of government. A precipitate of freedom and equality, it should be left to their devices. "I think the best remedy," Jefferson said, "is exactly that provided by all our constitutions, to leave the citizens the free election and separation of the aristoi from the pseudo-aristoi, of the wheat from the chaff. In general they will elect the real good and wise." He went on to speak of his revolutionary laws in Virginia abolishing entail and primogeniture, which "laid the axe to the root of pseudo-aristocracy," and of what remained to be done to complete the work. The counties should be divided into wards—a Virginia equivalent of New England townships—to collect the will of the people at the grassroots, and the people should be educated on the plan he had first proposed in 1778 partly with the view "of qualifying them to select the veritable aristoi." The Americans were not under the constraint of European theories of government, he told Adams. There was no canaille in America. "Here every one may have land to labor for himself. . . . Every one, by his property, or by his satisfactory situation, is interested in the support of law and order. And such men may safely and advantageously reserve to themselves a wholesome control over their public affairs."[39] Without exactly saying so, Jefferson suggested that Adams' political theory belonged to the Old World.

Adams, in reply, rejected Jefferson's basic distinction. The natural and the pseudo-aristocracy are one and the same, and every aristocracy tends to become hereditary. Who is an aristocrat? Every man, Adams answered, who commands one vote in addition to his own, whether this influence comes by way of birth, talent, beauty, fortune, or cunning. The definition was worse than useless, yet it struck closer to what Adams had been attempting to say on the subject of aristocracy than analogies to European nobility. His *bête noire,* as always, was equality. As there was no natural equality, so there could be no natural aristocracy in Jefferson's rarified sense. "Birth and wealth are conferred on some men, as imperiously by nature, as genius, strength or beauty." [40] After all, men are *born*, a fact of nature, into aristocratic families. Besides, every law providing for the descent of property militates against equality and ensures the perpetuation of aristocracy. Adams elaborated at length on these matters in a series of some thirty letters to Jefferson's Virginia friend, John Taylor of Caroline, whose *Inquiry into the Principles and Policy of the Government of the United States*, published in 1814, was a belated answer, tedious but effective, to Adams' *Defence*. [41] In 1820 Adams sat in the Massachusetts convention to revise the constitution he had himself drafted forty years before. The restricted suffrage came under attack and, in particular, reformers assailed the property basis of the senate as "an aristocratical principle." Tottering under the weight of eighty-five years, Adams rose to defend it. The great object of government being the security of property, he said, it must be shielded from the tyranny of numbers. Had not Aristides upset the balance of property in Athens, loosing the torrent of popular commotion that desolated the republic? Had not the French Revolution been doomed from the start by the adoption of the erroneous idea of government in one assembly? [42]

Adams was a voice from the past, while Jefferson continued to voice the aspirations, the rising aspirations, of American democracy. Still angry at Virginia's Constitution of 1776, trying it by "the mother principle, that 'governments are republican only in proportion as they embody the will of the people, and execute it,' " he proposed a comprehensive agenda of reform: universal white manhood suffrage, equality of representation, public education and similar measures to ensure "the ascendancy of the people." In the Massachusetts convention, Adams praised the work of "our ancestors," of whom he, strangely, was one, and doubted that a later generation could improve on it. In Virginia, Jefferson denounced "sanctimonious reverence" for institutions handed down from the past as an obstacle to the ongoing process of revision and reform that was vital to a free and enlightened society. Laws and institutions, he said, "must go hand in hand with the progress of the human mind." "We might as well require a man to wear still the coat which fitted him when a boy, as civilized society to remain ever under the regimen of their barbarous ancestors." [43] Partly because he held such opinions, no convention would be called to reform the Virginia Constitution until he was safely in his grave.

The question of progress, specifically, the progress of virtue, intelligence, and freedom, was a persistent theme in the correspondence from beginning to end. Looking back on the eighteenth century, Adams pronounced it good, more enlightened and more honorable to human nature than any other; yet it had ended in the disaster of the French Revolution, which exceeded even his darkest forebodings, and he sniffed reaction in the winds of change in the nineteenth century. Again and again he taunted Jefferson on the exploded hopes of the French Revolution. "Let me ask you, very seriously my friend, Where are now . . . the perfection and perfectibility of human nature? Where is now, the progress of the human mind? Where is the amelioration of society?" [44] Jefferson conceded that Adams had been the better prophet *so far*. The melancholy events of 1815, the return of the Bourbons, the Congress of Vienna, the Holy Alliance, wrote *finis* to the epoch of European liberty commenced so gloriously in 1789. Even Jefferson was led to question the first article of his faith. "I fear," he observed sadly to another friend, "from the experience of the last 25 years that morals do not, of necessity, advance hand in hand with the sciences." [45] Still, he could not rest in darkness and doubt. In the longer race of history, he told Adams, the cause of liberty and self-government would prevail, though "rivers of blood must yet flow, and years of desolation pass over." It had failed in the first attempt in Europe in part because of the ignorance, poverty, and vice of the mass of people, and because, as Adams also said, their leaders sought to scale the heights of liberty in one great leap. "But the world will recover from the panic of the first catastrophe. Science is progressive, and talents and enterprise on the alert." The idea of free government had taken root. Even kings must now honor it. "Opinion is power, and that opinion will come," Jefferson declared.[46]

Adams wanted to believe this, but where Jefferson was characteristically sanguine, concluding every expression of disappointment or doubt with an affirmation, the New Englander maintained his reputation for historical pessimism. When would the bloody circle of despotism, revolutionary democracy, anarchy, and returning despotism be broken? When would reason and conscience, however much improved by education and religion, ever prove a match for human passions? [47] About the French Revolution, the old friends could never agree. What a great *bouleversement* it had been! But who was most responsible for that? Jefferson asked. And he answered, the European despots who conspired against it and who even now quaked on their thrones. Adams, on the other hand, still inclined to blame the catastrophe of the revolution, not on its avowed enemies, but on its misguided prophets, those *philosophes*, so learned but destitute of common sense, preaching the perfectibility of mankind yet knowing nothing of men, whose books he could not read without imprecations—"poisonous stuff," "mad rant," "stark mad," "Fool! Fool!"—on his lips.[48] Nor could he find any redeeming virtues in the French Revolution. In 1815, however, with the Congress of Vienna, the seat of danger shifted from the revolutionary left to the reactionary right: from atheists to priests, from Jacobins to kings, from the prophets of progress to the prophets of a new dark age. "Priests and Politicians," Adams wrote, "never before, so suddenly and unanimously, concurred in establishing darkness and ignorance, superstition and despotism."[49] He referred to the so-called Holy Alliance, of course, but also to the restoration of the Society of Jesus, which revived in Adams old Puritan feelings about Roman Catholicism.

The age of revolution ended in the Latin American struggles for liberation. Neither Adams nor Jefferson was optimistic about the prospects of republican government in these countries sunk in ignorance, poverty, and superstition. For Adams the project was utterly chimerical, because "a free government and the Roman Catholic religion can never exist together in any nation or country."[50] Without entering into this prejudice, Jefferson called for the introduction of freedom and enlightenment by degrees, on a moderate plan such as he had recommended at the onset of the French Revolution. The Latin American revolutions led him to envision a hemispheric "American system" separated from the Old World and presided over by the republican genius of the United States. "What a Colossus shall we be when the Southern continent comes up to our mark!" he exclaimed to Adams in 1816. "What a stand will it secure as a ralliance for the reason and freedom of the globe."[51] The Monroe Doctrine seven years later gave a kind of diplomatic recognition to the idea.

Regardless of the fate of republicanism to the south, Jefferson looked upon the maturing United States as a well-lit fortress of freedom in an Atlantic world swept by reaction. "Must we," Adams asked once again in 1821, "before we take our departure from this good and beautiful world, surrender all our pleasing hopes of the progress of society? Of improvement . . . , of the reformation of mankind?"[52] Thinking of the struggles of the Greeks, of the Spaniards and the Italians against the antirevolutionary coalition in Europe, Jefferson admitted the horizon was clouded. "Yet I will not believe our labors are lost," he told Adams. "I shall not die without a hope that light and liberty are on steady advance. . . . And even should the cloud of barbarism and despotism again obscure the science and liberties of Europe, this country remains to preserve and restore light and liberty to them. In short, the flames kindled on the 4th of July 1776 have spread over too much of the globe to be extinguished by the feeble engines of despotism. On the contrary they will consume those engines, and all who work them." [53]

And so, it all came back finally to the American Revolution as the hope of the world. "Who shall write the history of the American revolution?" Adams queried his friend. "Who can write it? Who will ever be able to write it?" [54] Its true history was lost forever; so many lies had already been written, so many bloated reputations—Franklin's, Washington's, yes, and Jefferson's too—monopolized the page that Adams almost despaired of the subject together with his own revolutionary fame. (Years earlier, he had prophesied to Rush: "The essence of the whole will be that Dr. Franklin's electrical rod smote the earth and out sprung General Washington. That Franklin electrified him with his rod—and thence forward these two conducted all the policy, negotiations, legislatures and wars.") [55] Adams attended to his reputation in private, occasionally public, letters, but declined to write history or more than a fragment of autobiography. Jefferson's course was much the same. As the revolutionary age faded into the past, the patriarchs were besieged with requests for recollections, information, and materials on the nation's founding. Each cooperated in his own fashion while discouraging hagiology. The true history of the Revolution was important, said Adams, not only for America but for all countries, primarily because its lessons were conservative and admonitory. It would teach mankind "that revolutions are no trifles; that they ought never to be undertaken rashly; nor without deliberate consideration and sober reflection; nor without a solid, immutable, eternal foundation of justice and humanity; nor without a people possessed of intelligence, fortitude, and integrity sufficient to carry them with steadiness, patience, and perseverance, through all the vicissitudes of fortune, the fiery trials and melancholy disasters they may encounter."[56] With this emphasis Adams wished to disentangle the American Revolution from the French and to call attention to what was sound and solid in American character long before independence was declared. Jefferson, with his idealism, tended to see the Revolution in terms of goals rather than of origins. It was progressive, unfolding in time; it concerned the "revolution of 1800," or of 1789, as well as of 1776, and could not be written without a view to the struggle of principle between the great political parties. The best known general history, John Marshall's five-volume *Life of Washington,* was a Federalist diatribe in Jefferson's opinion. What he thought of Mercy Warren's spirited work, which caused Adams so much grief, is not known, but he remained anxious for a Republican historian to combat Marshall. None materialized.

Jefferson pressed the claims of Virginia, Adams those of Massachusetts, to precedence in the leadership of the Revolution. Although he thought William Wirt's biography of Patrick Henry "too flowery for the sober taste of history," he credited the Virginia Demosthenes with "setting the ball of revolution in motion." Adams waged a one-man campaign on behalf of James Otis, who did his work while Jefferson was still a boy in college, as the "Father of the American Revolution."[57] Jefferson's revolutionary fame soared with the fame of the Declaration of Independence now, in the exuberant patriotism following the War of 1812, celebrated as the very ark and covenant of the nation. "The mighty Jefferson, by his Declaration of Independence, 4 July 1776, carried away the glory both of the great and the little," Adams noted mournfully. "Such are the caprices of fortune."[58] It was thus with some pleasure that he called Jefferson's attention to the so-called Mecklenburg (North Carolina) Declaration of Independence of May 20, 1775, which came to light in 1819. Not only had it preceded the congressional declaration by over thirteen months, but the language of this relic plainly suggested that Jefferson was guilty of plagiarism. The reply came posthaste from Monticello: the document was a fabrication. Adams, who had at first supposed it genuine, promptly accepted Jefferson's verdict, which eventually became the verdict of history. In all these matters touching the history of the American Revolution, Adams and Jefferson were entirely amiable, and neither man placed the subject high on the agenda of discussion.

Old men, trying to transcend the past, they were more interested in religion than in history. Differences of religious belief, including different attitudes toward the role of religion in government, had helped to distinguish their politics, but as they grew older their religious convictions tended to converge. Jefferson became a kind of Christian humanist, a disciple of the morals of Jesus, while Adams "read himself out of bigotry," as he said, and embraced the Enlightenment's faith in reason. The Virginian's 1803 letter to Priestley, appearing in the London *Memoirs of Lindsey*, precipitated a wide-ranging discussion of religion. In that letter Jefferson had sketched the plan of a comparative view of the moral doctrines of the ancients, the Jews, and Jesus. He had hoped that Priestley would undertake this work. The great philosopher-theologian died within a few months, though not before he had dashed off *The Doctrines of Heathen Philosophy Compared with Revelation* in partial response to Jefferson's request. Adams now, in 1813, urged his friend to take up the work on his own account. He declined anything so thorny or ambitious, but told Adams that he had, just after his letter to Priestley, written a brief syllabus of the proposed inquiry, a copy of which he enclosed in strictest confidence. This "Syllabus of an Estimate of the Merit of the Doctrines of Jesus, Compared with Those of Others" reached the conclusion that the moral system of Jesus, if filled up in his spirit, would be "the most perfect and sublime" ever taught by man. The ancient heathen moralists, who had earlier won his allegiance, Jefferson now found deficient on several counts. So

far as they aimed at "tranquility of mind," they were great, and
Jefferson, who never ceased calling himself an Epicurean, continued to seek their instruction. But Jesus had pushed his
scrutinies into the recesses of the human heart, raised the
standard of universal philanthropy, and by his teaching of a
future state of rewards and punishments provided a powerful
incentive to moral conduct. Unfortunately, falling a victim to
"the combination of the altar and the throne," Jesus had been
unable to perfect his system; and it was mutilated and corrupted by the Platonizing priests and metaphysicians who pretended to be his followers.[59] The next step in Jefferson's plan
was to extract the pure from the impure in the gospels. He did
this to his own satisfaction, as he later explained to Adams,
by taking a New Testament, cutting from the books of the
evangelists only those verses that had the authentic stamp of
Jesus' genius, "as easily distinguished as diamonds in a dung-
hill," and arranging the whole into a text of forty-six pages
which he named "The Philosophy of Jesus."[60]

"Sancte Socrate! Ora pro nobis," Adams exclaimed. The
Syllabus proved that Jefferson was as good a Christian as
Priestley and most Unitarians, himself among them.[61] Jefferson thought so too. "I am a Christian in the only sense he
[Jesus] wished any one to be, sincerely attached to his doctrines, in preference to all others; ascribing to himself every
human excellence, and believing he never claimed any
other."[62] Whether this made Jefferson a Christian in any ac-
ceptable theological sense, including the Unitarian, may be
questioned. Priestley, in writing to Lindsey, had classified him
as an "unbeliever," though one who was "almost with us."[63]
Jefferson did not care; the only test of religion was conduct,
and so the moral branch alone concerned him. The republica-
tion of his letter to Priestley in a Boston volume, *American
Unitarianism*, in 1815, contributed to the rumors that he had
changed his religious opinions and planned to write a Christian confession of faith. Jefferson denied any material change;

as for writing a book on religion, he would as soon write for "the reformation of Bedlam." A sect unto himself, he still rejected revelation, the divinity of Christ, the miracles, the atonement, and so on, without which Christianity was nothing in the eyes of most believers. Few Unitarians cared to claim the reputed infidel one of them. He did not even accept Jesus on his own terms, for Jesus was a spiritualist by the grace of God, Jefferson a naturalist by the grace of science. But he had brought the morals of Jesus, above all the love of man, within the perimeters of the older faith of the Enlightenment. Returning to primitive Christianity, he had found in the teachings of Jesus a hard core of morality which infused a universal ethic based on the natural rights of man and around which, he thought, all men might be united in a common religion of humanity.

Adams applauded Jefferson's work and agreed with most of it. He had generally been more liberal in religion than in politics. His church in Quincy had been among the first to move away from Congregational orthodoxy and to adopt the Unitarian creed. He was a zealot, not about any particular creed, but about religion. It was in his blood and had weighed on his mind all his life. In matters of theology, especially Christian but not excepting the Hindu and other religions, he was better read than Jefferson, who had little taste for the subject and felt more comfortable resting his head on "that pillow of ignorance which the benevolent Creator has made so soft for us knowing how much we should be forced to use it." [64] In New England religion was a sober subject, to be approached in a sober manner; but in addressing Jefferson, Adams freed himself from these customary restraints and conversed with wild abandon. Speculations about God and eternity, matter and spirit, priests, saints, and demons were, he said, "the marbles and nine pins of old age," and in these games he found more amusement than any other.[65] He shared Jefferson's confidence in historical criticism as the way to recover religious

truth from the mountain of error built up by priests and
theologians. He did not know whether to laugh or cry over the
rising wave of evangelical Protestantism in the United States.
Observing the missionary appeal of the newly formed American Bible Society in 1816, Adams remarked, "Would it not
be better, to apply these pious subscriptions, to purify Chris-
tendom from the corruptions of Christianity, rather than to
propagate these corruptions in Europe, Asia, Africa, and
America!"[66] And after reading Dupuis on cults and impostures, he was often on the point of breaking out, "This would
be the best of all possible worlds, if there were no religion in
it."[67] But he could not. Even Dupuis, Adams told another
correspondent—interestingly, not Jefferson—had not shaken
his belief that Christianity was a revelation.[68] This belief, however rationalistic and moralistic Adams' sense of revelation,
continued to differentiate his religion from Jefferson's. The
argument that revelation was necessary to Christianity, according to the latter, gave a handle to atheism, for five-sixths of
mankind had no knowledge of it; it was, in truth, unnecessary
because the evidence of design in the universe and the moral
sense in man proved the existence of a beneficent first cause.
Adams declined to argue the point. There were certain questions, such as the divinity of Christ, upon which he did not care
to speculate. He was most at odds with Jefferson on the issue of
materialism and spiritualism. All the wearisome writings of
philosophers and theologians had convinced Adams that mortal man could know nothing of either matter or spirit. Jefferson
conceded the difficulty but, proceeding from Lockian sensa-
tionalism, referred to the experiments of certain scientists who
had recently shown that the thinking power of man, the spirit
or soul, was a function of matter inseparable from the body.
Matter was everything. "To talk of immaterial existences is to
talk of *nothings*. To say that the human soul, angels, god, are
immaterial is to say they are *nothings*, so that there is no god, no
angels, no soul."[69] This was Priestleyan as well as Lockian.

Adams, too, though he preached the widest latitude of religious freedom, remained committed to the system of compulsory tax-supported churches in Massachusetts, which survived the convention of 1820. Nevertheless, he could unite with Jefferson on a rational and moralistic religious creed, summed up in four short words, "Be just and good." [70]

As the years passed and both men pondered Cicero's *De Senectute*, the toll of physical affliction rose. Exchanging notes on their health in 1822, Jefferson said he could walk no farther than his garden, though he rode horseback every day, read without difficulty, and wrote his own letters despite the pain from an old wrist dislocation. Adams could not ride but walked easily enough, and he could neither read nor write for himself. At least they weren't "dying at the top." Their minds remained sound and active. Adams found happiness and contentment during these last years. While of comparatively modest means, he had no financial worries. Not since 1776 had he felt so hopeful for the American republic; indeed, in this regard, he seemed to revert to his earlier self. He had lost his wife in 1818, a terrible loss, and, like Jefferson, borne his share of family grief; but he had the infinite satisfaction of seeing his son John Quincy become president of the United States. A child of Jefferson's conception, the University of Virginia, gave him satisfaction of another kind; still, it could not dispel the gloom and disaster that gathered around him. With the Panic of 1819, his estate, long ravaged by debt, was drowned in it, and he was finally reduced to the humiliation of begging the favor of the legislature to dispose of most of his property by a lottery in the expectation—alas, not to be fulfilled—of saving the splendid monument, Monticello, for his daughter. The anguish of his personal affairs was enmeshed in political fears of sectional discord and neo-Federalist consolidation in the government at Washington. The Missouri Question in 1820, raising the claim of congressional jurisdiction to legislate on slavery in the territories, focused these fears. "From the battle of Bunker's hill to the treaty of Paris we never had so ominous a question," Jefferson told his friend.[71] He foresaw not only a renewal of the old party conflict, but a conflict now fanaticized by sectionalism. The Missouri Compromise, while it resolved the immediate crisis, drew a geographical line between slavery and freedom, which, he predicted, would become a constant irritant, stirring hatreds and fears, North and South, that must eventually terminate in disunion. Repeatedly during his public life Jefferson had attempted to find some solution to the problem of slavery. He still adhered to the plan of gradual emancipation framed for Virginia during the Revolution. But he no longer held much hope for it. One thing was clear: slavery could not be abolished by congressional fiat without destroying the Union and much else that was dear. "Are our slaves to be presented with freedom and a dagger?" he asked.[72] Adams was sympathetic. The Union held the first place in his political affections; and he had never thought that slavery, as hateful as it was, ranked with other evils facing the country. It must be left to the South, he wrote reassuringly. "I will vote for forcing no measure against your judgments."[73]

The Missouri Compromise was only the most dangerous part of the movement toward consolidation—protective tariff, national bank, internal improvements—that caused Jefferson to wonder if all the sacrifices he and Adams and the generation of 1776 had made for their country would be thrown away by their children. With respect to political temperament, the two men seemed to change places. Adams was serene, Jefferson morbid. The New Englander found the path of tranquility Jefferson had pointed out to him, while he, the Virginian, lost it in the gloom that invaded a declining society. Curiously, the latter's fears came to be projected on John Quincy Adams. During the prolonged contest that culminated in his election to the presidency, there was published a confidential correspondence between his father and the late William Cunningham in the early years of the century. The elder Adams' letters bristled with unflattering remarks on democracy and its idol, Jefferson. The object of the publication, for which Cunningham's son bore the responsibility, was to discredit the younger Adams by attempting to show that the elder had been the prolific fountain of Federalist abuse of Jefferson and, further, that the conversion of both father and son to Republicanism was a fraudulent disguise to cover their real purpose of raising an aristocratic family dynasty in the American government. Beware, the younger Cunningham warned the public, of engrafting "a Scion of this old Stock in our tree of liberty." [74] The Cunningham correspondence did little damage to John Quincy Adams, but it caused considerable embarrassment to his father. Jefferson, sensing the embarrassment, at once addressed Adams a letter denouncing this "outrage on private confidence," this poisonous attack on their affections. "Be assured, my dear Sir, that I am incapable of receiving the slightest impression from the effort now made to plant thorns on the pillow of age, worth, and wisdom, and to sow tares between friends who have been such for near half a century." [75] Adams rejoiced: "The best letter that ever was written. . . . How generous! how noble! how magnanimous!" [76] Jefferson could sincerely felicitate Adams on his son's election, though he had backed another candidate; but the new president's enunciation of a boldly nationalistic program transported Jefferson back to the Federalist decade. He gave aid and comfort to Virginia's "old" Republicans laboring to revive the individualistic and state rights "doctrines of '98." He lashed out at the new breed of Republicans, products of nationalizing forces he had himself stimulated, but who "having nothing in them of the principles of '76 now look back to a single and splendid government of an aristocracy, founded on banking institutions and monied incorporations . . . riding and ruling over the plundered ploughman and beggared yeomanry." And, he added, should it finally settle down to the alternatives of "dissolution of our Union . . . or submission to a government

without limitation of powers," there could be no hesitation in
the choice of liberty.[77] Thus this rebel against the past came to
the end of his days haunted by demons he had vanquished a
quarter-century before, while Adams, so long in political torment, rested peacefully, securely, at the homestead he now
jokingly called Montezillo.

->>><<<-

The venerable sages of Monticello and Montezillo died on the
fiftieth anniversary of American independence, July 4, 1826.
It was a day of jubilee all across the land. Both the patriarchs, in
their last illnesses, had prayed to live to see the day. Adams,
declining an invitation to attend the celebration in Quincy,
called the American Revolution "a memorable epoch in the
annals of the human race," and, always the monitor, said it was
destined to form "the brightest or the blackest page" in history
depending on the use or abuse of the legacy by posterity.[78]
Jefferson, equally in character to the end, summoned all his
eloquence to pen a bold last testament to the American people
in a letter addressed to the observance in Washington. "All eyes
are opened, or opening, to the rights of man. The general
spread of the light of science has already laid open to every
view the palpable truth, that the mass of mankind has not been
born with saddles on their backs, nor the favored few booted
and spurred, ready to ride them legitimately, by the grace of
God."[79]

The passing of these two political fathers on the day of jubilee, a coincidence so remarkable it could only be explained as
providential, led to an American apotheosis, not alone of the
dead, but of the nation's revolutionary epoch.[80] In solemn
commemorations from the Atlantic to the Mississippi, Americans raised an anthem of praise to Adams and Jefferson. Providence, it was said, had decreed by their death that "the revolutionary age should be closed up." Suddenly, self-consciously,
the nation recognized it had a past, a golden age, a glorious

heritage, complete with heroes and scriptures to guide its footsteps toward a more glorious destiny. Eulogists such as Daniel Webster discovered striking parallels in the lives of Adams and Jefferson, giving the impression of a surpassing harmony of purpose; and some placed their "sublime example" of reunion "at the head of their catalogue of praises" because of what it signified for the American Union. In them Massachusetts and Virginia, North and South, were one. Still, as an old Federalist remarked, their tempers and politics were such as would at one time have made "a very tolerable salad," and it could never have occurred to partisans of one or the other in 1800 that it would ultimately end in one homogenous mixture admitting one and the same apotheosis. Harmony was the eulogists' motif, but they did not fail to observe the contrasting meanings of Adams and Jefferson for the nation. Adams was Roman, Jefferson was Grecian; Adams was a realist, Jefferson an idealist; Adams trusted the lessons of the past, Jefferson dreamed of the future; Adams was a Whig of the old school, Jefferson belonged to the modern democratic school; Adams advocated restraints on the popular will, Jefferson advocated its ascendancy. All of this was true, more or less, and the contrasting idioms of the two men entered into the political dialogue of the future. But Adams and Jefferson, philosophical statesmen in an age of revolution, were more comparable to each other than they were to the leaders of a new and brassy age regardless of political persuasions.

Although Adams died five hours after his Virginia friend, his last words, "Thomas Jefferson still survives," uttered a truth beyond their literal error. Jefferson lived on in American spirit because his thought, not just in politics but in most of the avenues of civilization, addressed the future. He became a symbol of American liberty, and a great memorial would finally be raised to him in the nation's capital. Even the denunciations and the demeanings, ever plentiful, contributed to keeping his memory green. It was Adams' fate, on the other hand, to be neglected by posterity, as he always knew he would be. "Mausoleums, statues, monuments will never be erected to me," he had prophesied in 1809, "nor flattering orations spoken to transmit me to posterity in brilliant colors."[81] Still, his influence survived, if not in the American spirit, then in American institutions, above all in the workings of constitutional government; and his thought, even when unrecognized as his, helped to keep the democracy born of Jefferson's vision alert to its own delusions and its suicidal tendencies. It was not a legacy, like Jefferson's, inspiring the hopes and dreams of mankind, but one for which Americans might also be grateful two hundred years after the nation's birth.

Notes

ONE—*The American Revolution*

1. Thomas Jefferson (TJ) to Francis Eppes, 26 June 1775, in Julian P. Boyd, ed., *The Papers of Thomas Jefferson*, 19 vols. to date (Princeton, N.J., 1950–), I, 174.

2. John Adams (JA) to James Lloyd, 29 March 1815, in Charles Francis Adams, ed., *The Works of John Adams*, 10 vols. (Boston, 1850–56), X, 149.

3. Benjamin Rush to JA, 17 February 1812, in John A. Schutz and Douglass Adair, eds., *The Spur to Fame: Dialogues of John Adams and Benjamin Rush, 1805–1813* (San Marino, Calif., 1966), p. 211n.

4. Daniel Webster, *A Discourse in Commemoration of the Lives and Services of John Adams and Thomas Jefferson* ... (Boston, 1826), p. 9.

5. TJ to Benjamin Rush, 16 January 1811, in Paul L. Ford, ed., *The Writings of Thomas Jefferson* (New York, 1892–99), IX 295–96.

6. Adams, ed., Autobiography, Diary, *Works*, II, 430.

7. Ibid., p. 514.

8. See William Peden, "Thomas Jefferson: Book Collector," (Ph.D. diss., University of Virginia, 1942); and Zoltán Haraszti, *John Adams and the Prophets of Progress* (Cambridge, Mass., 1952).

9. George A. Peek, Jr., ed., *The Political Writings of John Adams* (New York, 1954), p. 7. And see Wesley Frank Craven, *The Legend of the Founding Fathers* (New York, 1956), pp. 23–27.

10. Adams, ed., Diary, *Works*, II, 250.

11. JA To Mercy Warren, 8 January 1776, in *Warren-Adams Letters, Being Chiefly a Correspondence among John Adams, and James Warren, 1743—1814*, 2 vols. (Boston, 1917–25), I, 201–2.

12. Boyd, ed., *Papers*, II, 545–46.

13. Mercy Warren to JA, 27 August 1807, in Charles Francis Adams, ed., "Correspondence between John Adams and Mercy Warren," *Collections of the Masachusetts Historical Society*, 5th series (1878), IV, 480.

14. JA to Mercy Warren, 25 November 1775, in Adams, ed., *Works*, IX, 368.

15. TJ to JA, 8 April 1816, in Lester J. Cappon, ed., *The Adams-Jefferson Letters* (Chapel Hill, N.C., 1959), p. 467.

16. JA to Abigail Adams, 3 August 1776, in Charles Francis Adams, ed.,

Familiar Letters of John Adams and His Wife Abigail Adams, During the Revolution (Boston, 1875), p. 207.

17. JA to Benjamin Rush, 27 February 1805, Schutz and Adair, eds., *Spur to Fame*, pp. 23–24.

18. Adams, ed., Diary, *Works*, II, 304, 63.

19. JA to Abigail Adams, 6 March 1777, Adams ed., *Familiar Letters*, p. 250.

20. JA to Abigail Adams, 18 August 1776, ibid., p. 214.

21. JA's views are most fully expounded in the *Novanglus* series, included in *Works*, IV.

22. Adams, ed., Diary, *Works*, II, 311–13; JA to John Winthrop, 23 June 1776, ibid. IX, 409–10.

23. Lyman C. Butterfield, ed., *The Diary and Autobiography of John Adams*, 4 vols. (Cambridge, Mass., 1961), III, 282–83.

24. Adams, ed., Notes on Debates, *Works*, II, 499–500.

25. TJ's work was written as proposed instructions for the Virginia delegates to the First Continental Congress and was published without his consent or ascription of authorship. The manuscript text may be found in Boyd, ed., *Papers*, I, 121–35. JA's *Novanglus* essays were first published in the *Boston Gazette*, December 1774–April 1775, in rebuttal of the essays of *Massachusettensis*, the Loyalist Daniel Leonard. See Adams, ed., *Works*, IV 3–180.

26. Boyd, ed., *Papers*, I, 122–23.

27. Ibid., I, 134.

28. Quoted in G. H. Guttridge, *English Whiggism and the American Revolution* (Berkeley, Calif., 1942), p. 62.

29. JA to Mercy Warren, 8 January 1776, *Warren-Adams Letters*, I, 201; JA to Abigail Adams, 18 February 1776, Adams, ed., *Familiar Letters*, pp. 134–35.

30. TJ to John Randolph, 25 August 1775, Boyd, ed., *Papers*, I, 242.

31. Adams, ed., Autobiography, *Works*, II, 508.

32. JA to Mercy Warren, 20 May 1776, *Warren-Adams Letters*, I, 249.

33. JA to Timothy Pickering, 6 August 1822, Adams, ed., *Works*, II, 512–14n. See also TJ to James Madison, 30 August 1823, Ford, ed., *Writings*, X, 267.

34. Ibid.

35. Ibid. TJ to W. P. Gardner, 19 February 1813, ibid., IX, 277–78.

36. JA to Abigail Adams, 3 July 1776, Adams, ed., *Works*, IX, 420.

37. *Thoughts on Government*, in Peek, ed., *Political Writings*, p. 92.

38. TJ to Thomas Nelson, 16 May 1776, Boyd, ed., *Papers*, I, 292.

39. JA to Mercy Warren, 16 April 1776, *Warren-Adams Letters*, I, 221; to Benjamin Franklin, 27 July 1784, Adams, ed., *Works*, VIII, 207–8; to James Warren, 17 July 1782, ibid., IX, 512; to Abigail Adams, 4 October 1776, Adams, ed., *Familiar Letters*, p. 231.

40. The *Thoughts on Government* may be conveniently found in Peek, ed., *Political Writings*, pp. 83–92. It is also in Adams, ed., *Works*, IV, 193–200.

41. JA to Samuel Adams, 10 October 1790, VI, 415.

42. Adams, ed., *Defence of the American Constitutions*, in *Works*, IV, 358; JA to Samuel Perley, 13 June 1809, ibid., IX, 621–24.

43. JA to Mercy Warren, 16 April 1776, *Warren-Adams Letters*, I, 222; to Joseph Hawley, 25 August 1776, Adams, ed., *Works*, IX, 433–35.

44. Adams Papers Microfilm, Miscellany (Massachusetts Historical Society); TJ to Peter Carr, 10 August 1787, Boyd, ed., *Papers*, XII, 14–15.

45. The three drafts of TJ's proposed constitution, together with the text adopted by the convention, are in Boyd, ed., *Papers*, I, 328–86. A later draft constitution, of 1783, was published as an appendix in TJ's *Notes on the State of Virginia* (London, 1787). See the edition by William Peden (Chapel Hill, N.C., 1954), pp. 109–22.

46. *Autobiography of Thomas Jefferson* (New York, 1959), p. 62.

47. TJ to Samuel Kercheval, 12 July 1816, Ford, ed., *Writings*, X, 37.

48. Adams, ed., *Works*, IV, 219–67, prints the constitution as reported and notes the changes made in the convention.

49. JA to James Sullivan, 26 May 1776, Adams, ed., *Works*, IX, 376.

50. Ibid.

51. JA to Benjamin Rush, 12 April 1809, ibid., IX, 618.

52. JA to Jebediah Morse, 29 November 1815, ibid., X, 182.

53. Philip S. Foner, *The Complete Writings of Thomas Paine*, 2 vols. (New York, 1945), I, 45.

TWO—*The French Revolution*

1. On the subject in general, see Gerald Stourzh, *Benjamin Franklin and American Foreign Policy* (Chicago, 1954); Felix Gilbert, *To the Farewell Address* (New York, 1961); Merrill D. Peterson, "Thomas Jefferson and American Commercial Policy, 1783–1793," in Peterson, ed., *Thomas Jefferson: A Profile* (New York, 1967), pp. 104–34.

2. See, for example, JA to James Warren, 13 April 1783, *Warren-Adams Letters*, II, 209–12.

3. JA to James Warren, 9 April 1783, ibid., II, 206. On JA's response to these events, see the discussion in John R. Howe, Jr., *The Changing Political Thought of John Adams* (Princeton, 1966), chap. 4.

4. JA to Robert R. Livingston, 5 February 1783, Adams, ed., *Works*, VIII, 35–40.

5. JA to John Jay, 13 April 1785, ibid., VIII, 234.

6. James Madison to TJ, 11 February, 6 May 1783, and TJ to James Madison, 14 February 1783, Boyd, ed., *Papers*, VI, 235, 265, 241.

7. JA to Robert R. Livingston, 21 February 1782, Adams, ed., *Works*, VII, 528.

8. TJ to Robert Walsh, 4 December 1818, in A. A. Lipscomb and A. E. Bergh, eds., *The Writings of Thomas Jefferson*, 20 vols. (Washington, 1903), XV, 176.

9. TJ to Lafayette, 2 April 1790, Boyd, ed., *Papers*, XVI, 293. Cf. TJ to James Madison, 28 August 1789, ibid., XV, 367.

10. JA to James Warren, 27 August 1784, Adams, ed., *Works*, IX, 524.

11. TJ to James Madison, 30 January 1787, Boyd, ed., *Papers*, IX, 94–95.

12. Abigail Adams to Mrs. Cranch, 8 May 1785, in Charles Francis Adams, ed., *Letters of Mrs. Adams*, 2 vols. (Boston, 1848), II, 94.

13. Abigail Adams to TJ, 6 June 1785, Cappon, ed., *Adams-Jefferson Letters*, p. 28.

14. JA to TJ, 4 September 1785, ibid., p. 61.

15. JA to TJ, 3 October 1785, ibid., p. 77.

16. TJ to Abigail Adams, 21 June 1785, ibid., p. 34.

17. TJ to John Page, 4 May 1786, Boyd, ed., *Papers*, IX, 446.

18. Butterfield, ed., *Diary and Autobiography*, III, 186. For TJ's "Notes of a Tour of English Gardens," see Boyd, ed., *Papers*, IX, 369–75.

19. "Observations on Demeunier's Manuscript," 28 October 1785, Boyd, ed., *Papers*, X, 52; TJ to James Monroe, 17 June 1785, ibid., VIII, 233.

20. JA to Lafayette, 12 May 1782, Adams, ed., *Works*, VII, 593. For the general subject, see Edward Handler, *America and Europe in the Political Thought of John Adams* (Cambridge, Mass., 1961).

21. Adams, ed., Diary and Autobiography, *Works*, III, 171; TJ to Charles Bellini, 30 September 1785, and to Eliza House Trist, 18 August 1785, Boyd, ed., *Papers*, VIII, 568–69, 404.

22. TJ to Charles Bellini, 30 September 1785, ibid., VIII, 569.

23. JA to Abigail Adams, 12 April 1778, Adams, ed., *Familiar Letters*, p. 329.

24. TJ to James Madison, 20 September 1785, Boyd, ed., *Papers*, VIII, 535.

25. JA to Abigail Adams, 1780, Adams, ed., *Familiar Letters*, p. 381.

26. Peter Gay, *The Enlightenment: An Interpretation*, 2 vols. (New York, 1968–69), II, 125.

27. JA to F. A. Van der Kemp, March 1804, Adams, ed., *Works*, IX, 380.

28. See the interesting character sketch in Mercy Warren, *History of the Rise, Progress and Termination of the American Revolution*, 3 vols. (Boston, 1805), III, 176–77.

29. The full title is *A Defence of the Constitutions of the Government of the United States of America against the attack of M. Turgot, in his letter to Dr. Price, dated the twenty-second of March, 1778*. It may be found in Adams, ed., *Works*, IV–VI, though with certain changes in the original text.

30. Letters to John Taylor, ibid., VI 489–90. This was written in 1814, but see also JA to Richard Cranch, 15 January 1787, to Reverend De Walter, October 1797, and to F. A. Van der Kemp, 20 January 1800, Adams Papers Microfilm, Letterbooks.

31. JA to TJ, 28 October 1787, Cappon, ed., *Adams-Jefferson Letters*, p. 204.

32. TJ to JA, 23 February 1787, ibid., pp. 174–75. About the subsequent volumes Jefferson had little to say except to wish that Adams had addressed himself to the problems of republican confederations. It seems quite likely that Jefferson gave only cursory reading at best to the second and third volumes, the last being the boldest of the three.

33. TJ to Abigail Adams, 22 February 1787, ibid., p. 173.

34. See Peden, ed., *Notes on Virginia*, p. 120.

35. JA to F. A. Van der Kemp, 27 March 1790, Adams Papers Microfilm, Letterbooks.

36. TJ to William S. Smith, 13 November 1787, Boyd, ed., *Papers*, XII, 357.

37. TJ to JA, 13 November 1787, Cappon, ed., *Adams-Jefferson Letters*, p. 212.

38. JA to TJ, 6 December 1787, ibid., pp. 213–14.

39. TJ's argument for a bill of rights is developed in letters to James Madison, 20 December 1787, 31 July 1788, and 15 March 1789, Boyd, ed., *Papers*, XII, 440, XIII, 442–43, XIV, 659–60.

40. JA to Richard Price, 19 April 1790, Adams, ed., *Works*, IX, 564.

41. TJ to JA, 28 September 1787, Cappon, ed., *Adams-Jefferson Letters*, pp. 199–200.

42. JA to John Jay, 23 September 1787, Adams, ed., *Works*, IX, 454.

43. JA to TJ, 9 October 1787, Cappon, ed., *Adams-Jefferson Letters*, pp. 202–3.

44. JA to Richard Price, 19 April 1790, Adams ed., *Works*, IX, 563.

45. *The Spirit of the Laws*, Walter Nugent, tr. (New York, 1949), 16. See the observations in Robert R. Palmer, *The Age of the Democratic Revolution*, 2 vols., (Princeton, 1959–64), I, 26; and also JA to Samuel Adams, 18 October 1790, Adams, ed., *Works*, VI, 416–17.

46. TJ to Anne Willing Bingham, 11 May 1788, Boyd, ed., *Papers*, XIII, 151.

47. TJ to Francis Hopkinson, 8 May 1788, ibid., XIII, 145.

48. TJ to Edward Rutledge, 18 July 1788, ibid,, XIII, 378.

49. TJ to St. John de Crèvecoeur, 9 August 1788, ibid., XIII, 485–86.

50. TJ to JA, 5 December 1788, Cappon, ed., *Adams-Jefferson Letters*, pp. 231–32.

51. "Draft of a Charter of Rights," [3 June 1789], Boyd, ed., *Papers*, XV, 167–68.

52. *Autobiography*, p. 163.

53. TJ to John Jay, 17 June 1789, Boyd, ed., *Papers*, XV, 189.

54. TJ to Diodati, 3 August 1789, ibid., XV, 325.

55. Ibid., p. 326.

56. See William Short to TJ, 6 March 1787, ibid., XI, 239–40.

57. Joyce Appleby, "The Jefferson-Adams Rupture and the First French Translation of John Adams' *Defence*," *American Historical Review*, vol. 63 (1968), pp. 1084–91. See also, on Jefferson and Montesquieu, Merrill D. Peterson, "Thomas Jefferson and the Enlightenment: Reflections on Literary Influence," *Lex et Scientia*, vol. XI (1975), pp. 89–127.

58. *Autobiography*, p. 114. See also Palmer, *Democratic Revolution*, I, chap. 15.

59. JA to Count Sarsfield, 16 September 1789, Adams Papers Microfilm, Letterbooks.

60. TJ to Lafayette, 2 April 1790, Boyd, ed., *Papers*, XVI, 293.

61. TJ to Diodati, 3 August 1789, ibid., XV, 326.

62. JA to George Washington, 17 May 1789, Adams, ed., *Works*, VIII, 493. Cf. JA to James Lovell, 16 July 1789, Adams Papers Microfilm, Letterbooks.

63. Adams, ed., Autobiography, *Works*, III, 175.

64. TJ to James Madison, 29 June 1789, Boyd, ed., *Papers*, XV, 315–16.

65. JA to Benjamin Rush, 9 July 1789, in Alexander Biddle, ed., *Old Family Letters* (Philadelphia, 1892), pp. 37–38.

66. JA to F. A. Van der Kemp, 27 March 1790, Adams Papers Microfilm, Letterbooks; JA to Roger Sherman, 18, 20 July 1789, Adams, ed., *Works*, VI, 430–36.

67. Warren, *History of the Revolution*, III, 393.

68. Benjamin Rush, *Autobiography*, George W. Corner, ed., (Princeton, 1948), p. 143; TJ, Anas (4 February 1818), in Lipscomb and Bergh, eds., *Writings*, I, 279–80.

69. Ibid., pp. 270–71.

70. In Adams, ed., *Works*, VI, 228–403.

71. Ibid., p. 276.

72. William Maclay, *Journal*, E. S. Maclay, ed. (New York, 1890), p. 243.

73. Foner, ed., *Writings of Paine*, I, 339.

74. See the note in Ford, ed., *Writings*, V, 354n.

75. TJ to George Washington, 8 May 1791, ibid., V, 328–29.

76. TJ to JA, 17 July 1791, Cappon, ed., *Adams-Jefferson Letters*, p. 246.

77. JA to TJ, 29 July 1791, ibid., pp. 247–50.

78. TJ to JA, 30 August 1791, ibid., pp. 250–51.

79. TJ to Thomas Paine, 19 June 1792, Ford, ed., *Writings*, VI, 88.

80. TJ to George Mason, 4 February 1791, ibid., V, 274–75; TJ to Sir John Sinclair, 24 August 1791, Lipscomb and Bergh, eds., *Writings*, VIII, 231.

81. Quoted in Page Smith, *John Adams*, 2 vols. (New York, 1962), II, 833.

82. JA to Benjamin Rush, 10 October 1808, Schutz and Adair, eds., *Spur to Fame*, pp. 122–23.

83. See, for example, JA to Benjamin Waterhouse, 21 May 1821, in Worthington C. Ford, ed., *Statesman and Friend: Correspondence of John Adams with Benjamin Waterhouse, 1784–1822* (Boston, 1927), p. 155.

84. TJ, Anas (4 February 1818), Lipscomb and Bergh, eds., *Writings*, I, 279.

THREE—*"The Revolution of 1800"*

1. JA to Tristram Dalton, 19 January 1797, Adams Papers Microfilm, Letterbooks.

2. See Noble E. Cunningham, Jr., *The Jeffersonian Republicans: The Formation of Party Organization, 1789–1801* (Chapel Hill, N.C., 1957), pp. 97–98.

3. See Manning J. Dauer, *The Adams Federalists* (Baltimore, 1953).

4. TJ to David Howell, 14 November 1793, Jefferson Papers Microfilm, Library of Congress; to Tench Coxe, 1 May 1794, Ford, ed., *Writings*, VI, 507–8.

5. Quoted in Smith, *John Adams*, II, 846.

6. TJ to James Madison, 21 September 1795, Ford, ed., *Writings*, VII, 32–33.

7. TJ to James Madison, 27 April 1795, ibid., VII, 10.

8. JA to Abigail Adams, 14 January 1797, Adams Papers Microfilm, Letterbooks.

9. TJ to JA, 25 April 1794, and JA to TJ, 11 May 1794, Cappon, ed., *Adams-Jefferson Letters*, pp. 253–55.

10. TJ to JA, 28 February 1796, ibid., p. 260.

11. TJ to James Madison, 17 December 1796, Ford, ed., *Writings*, VII, 91–92.

12. James Madison to TJ, 19 December 1796, in Gaillard Hunt, ed., *Writings of James Madison*, 9 vols. (New York, 1900–1910), VI, 301–2; Benjamin Rush to TJ, 4 January 1797, Jefferson Papers Microfilm.

13. Alexander Hamilton to Rufus King, 15 February 1797, in Charles R. King, ed., *Life and Correspondence of Rufus King*, 6 vols. (New York, 1894–1900), II, 148.

14. TJ to JA, 28 December 1796, Cappon, ed., *Adams-Jefferson Letters*, pp. 262–63.

15. TJ to James Madison, 1 January 1797, Ford, ed., *Writings*, V, 99.

16. James Madison to TJ, 15 January 1797, Hunt, ed., *Madison Writings*, VI, 302–4; TJ to James Madison, 30 January 1797, Ford, ed., *Writings*, VII, 115–16.

17. *Boston Patriot* articles, 1809, in Adams, ed., *Works*, IX, 284–85.

18. Ibid., p. 286.

19. Anas (2 March 1797), Lipscomb and Bergh, eds., *Writings*, I, 415.

20. Adams, ed., *Works*, IX, 105–10.

21. Special Message, 16 May 1797, ibid., pp. 110–15.

22. TJ to Elbridge Gerry, 13 May 1797, Ford, ed., *Writings*, VII, 121–22.

23. JA to Elbridge Gerry, 13 February 1797, to Oliver Wolcott, 27 October 1797, Adams, ed., *Works*, VIII, 523, 559; and to Gerry, 3 May 1797, Adams Papers Microfilm, Letterbooks.

24. TJ to Elbridge Gerry, 13 May 1797, Ford, ed., *Writings*, VII, 120.

25. JA to Tristram Dalton, 19 January 1797, and to Elbridge Gerry, 20 February 1797, Adams Papers Microfilm, Letterbooks.

26. TJ to Philip Mazzei, 24 April 1796, Ford, ed., *Writings*, VII, 75–76.

27. Uriah Forrest to JA, June 1797, Adams Papers Microfilm; JA to Uriah Forrest, 20 June 1797, Adams, ed., *Works*, VIII, 546–47.

28. Quoted in Smith, *John Adams*, II, 940.

29. TJ to Thomas Mann Randolph, 3 May 1798, Jefferson Papers Microfilm.

30. Adams, ed., *Works*, IX, 193, 202.

31. Ibid., p. 229.

32. Ibid., pp. 182, 195.

33. TJ to James Madison, 3 May 1798, Ford, ed., *Writings*, VII, 247.

34. Adams, ed., *Works*, IX, 192, 205, 196.

35. James Madison to TJ, 13 May 1798, in *Letters and Other Writings of James Madison*, 4 vols. (Washington, D.C., 1894), II, 140.

36. Adams, ed., Addresses, *Works*, IX, 187.

37. JA to TJ, 30 June 1813, Cappon, ed., *Adams-Jefferson Letters*, p. 347.

38. TJ to Thomas Mann Randolph, 3 May 1798, Jefferson Papers Microfilm; TJ to François d'Ivernois, 6 February 1795, Lipscomb and Bergh, eds., *Writings*, IX, 297–98.

39. TJ to Elbridge Gerry, 26 January 1799, Ford, ed., *Writings*, VII, 328–29.

40. TJ to JA, 15 June 1813, Cappon, ed., *Adams-Jefferson Letters*, p. 332.

41. TJ to Thomas Mann Randolph, 9 May 1798, Jefferson Papers Microfilm.

42. TJ to Edward Carrington, 16 January 1787, Boyd, ed., *Papers*, XI, 49.

43. TJ to James Madison, 28 December 1794, Ford, ed., *Writings*, VI, 516–17.

44. Quoted in Smith, *John Adams*, II, 865.

45. Richard Hildreth, *The History of the United States*, 2d ser., 3 vols. (New York, 1851), II, 161; TJ to James Monroe, 7 September 1797, Ford, ed., *Writings*, VII, 172–73.

46. JA to Timothy Pickering, 16 September 1798, Adams, ed., *Works*, VIII, 596.

47. JA to James McHenry, 22 October 1798, ibid., VIII, 613.

48. TJ to John Taylor, 1 June 1798, Ford, ed., *Writings*, VII, 265.

49. TJ to S. T. Mason, 11 October 1798, ibid., VII, 283.

50. TJ's draft together with the resolutions as adopted are in ibid., pp. 287–309.

51. TJ to James Madison, 26 February 1799, ibid., VII, 370.

52. Ibid.

53. JA to George Washington, 19 February 1799, to John Marshall, 4 September 1800, Adams, ed., *Works*, VIII, 626; IX, 80–81.

54. JA to James Lloyd, 30 March 1815, ibid., X, 151.

55. JA to James McHenry, 27 July 1799, ibid., IX, 4–5.

56. Timothy Pickering to Rufus King, 20 May 1800, King, ed., *Correspondence*, II, 248.

57. See Gabriel Duval to James Madison, 17 October 1800, Madison Papers Microfilm, Library of Congress.

58. In Seth Ames, ed., *Works of Fisher Ames*, 2 vols. (Boston, 1854), II, 115.

59. Alexander Hamilton to John Jay, 7 May 1800, in Henry Cabot Lodge, ed., *The Works of Alexander Hamilton*, 12 vols. (New York, 1904), X, 372.

60. TJ to Benjamin Rush, 16 January 1811, Ford, ed., *Writings*, IX, 295.

61. What follows is drawn primarily from TJ to Elbridge Gerry, 26 January 1799, ibid., VII, 328–29, but see also TJ to Gideon Granger, 13 August 1800, ibid., pp. 450–53.

62. TJ to John Breckinridge, 29 January 1800, ibid., p. 418.

63. JA to Elbridge Gerry, 30 December 1800, Adams, ed., *Works*, IX, 555.

64. Anas (15 April 1806), Lipscomb and Bergh, eds., *Writings*, I, 451–52; cf. JA to Elbridge Gerry, 7 February 1801, Adams, ed., *Works*, IX, 97.

65. Ford, ed., *Writings*, VIII, 1–6.

66. TJ to Spencer Roane, 6 September 1819, ibid., IX, 140.

67. JA to William Cunningham, 15 March 1804, in *Correspondence between the Hon. John Adams and the Late William Cunningham, Esq.* (Boston, 1823), p. 19.

68. JA to Benjamin Waterhouse, 22 May 1815, Ford, ed., *Statesman and Friend*, p. 116.

FOUR—*Retrospect and Prospect*

1. JA to Daniel Wright and Erastus Lyman, 13 March 1809, Adams, ed., *Works*, IX, 613–15. See also JA to Benjamin Rush, 12 April 1809, ibid., pp. 616–19.

2. JA to Benjamin Rush, 23 March 1809, 16 September 1810, Schutz and Adair, eds., *Spur to Fame*, pp. 139, 168; Josiah Quincy, *Figures of the Past* (Boston, 1883), p. 78.

3. Charles Francis Adams, ed., "Correspondence between John Adams and Mercy Warren," *Collections of the Massachusetts Historical Society*, 5th ser. (1878), IV, 317–511.

4. JA to James Lloyd, 6 February 1815, Adams, ed., *Works*, X, 115.

5. JA to James Lloyd, January 1815, ibid., p. 113.

6. TJ to Abigail Adams, 13 June 1804, Cappon, ed., *Adams-Jefferson Letters*, p. 270.

7. Abigail Adams to TJ, 1 July 1804, ibid., p. 274.

8. TJ to Abigail Adams, 22 July 1804, ibid., p. 275.

9. Abigail Adams to TJ, 25 October 1804, ibid., pp. 281–82.

10. See JA to William Cranch, 20 May 1801, to F. A. Van der Kemp, 5 November 1804, and to Thomas Truxtun, 13 December 1804, Adams Papers Microfilm, Letterbooks.

11. See JA to William Cunningham, 27 September 1808, *Adams-Cunningham Correspondence*, pp. 25–26.

12. JA to Benjamin Rush, 6 February 1805, Schutz and Adair, eds., *Spur to Fame*, p. 21.

13. JA to William Cunningham, 16 January 1804, *Adams-Cunningham Correspondence*, p. 11.

14. TJ to Abigail Adams, 11 September 1804, Cappon, ed., *Adams-Jefferson Letters*, p. 280.

15. See, for example, JA to J. B. Varnum, 26 December 1808, Adams, ed., *Works*, IX, 605–8.

16. JA to Benjamin Waterhouse, 12 July 1811, Ford, ed., *Statesman and Friend*, p. 64.

17. TJ to Benjamin Rush, 16 January 1811, Ford, ed., *Writings*, IX, 295–99.

18. Edward Coles to Henry S. Randall, 11 May 1857, in Randall, *Life of Thomas Jefferson*, 3 vols. (Philadelphia, 1857), III, 639–40.

19. Benjamin Rush to JA, 16 December 1811, in Lyman Butterfield, ed., *The Letters of Benjamin Rush*, 2 vols. (Princeton, 1951), II, 110.

20. JA to Benjamin Rush, 25 December 1811, Adams, ed., *Works*, X, 11–12.

21. JA to TJ, 1 January 1812 and TJ to JA, 21 January 1812, Cappon, ed., *Adams-Jefferson Letters*, pp. 290–92.

22. TJ to JA, 27 June 1822, ibid., p. 581.

23. JA to TJ, 2 February 1817, ibid., p. 507.

24. JA to TJ, 25 December 1813, ibid., p. 409.

25. TJ to JA, 27 June 1813, ibid., p. 337.

26. JA to TJ, 12 July 1813, ibid., p. 354.

27. JA to TJ, 11 January 1817, ibid., p. 505.

28. TJ to JA, 21 January 1812, ibid., p. 291.

29. TJ to JA, 11 June 1812, ibid., p. 308.

30. JA to TJ, 28 June 1813, ibid., p. 311.

31. TJ to JA, 27 May 1813, ibid., p. 324.

32. TJ to Joseph Priestley, 21 March 1801, Ford, ed., *Writings*, VIII, 21.

33. JA to TJ, 29 May, 10 June 1813, Cappon, ed., *Adams-Jefferson Letters*, pp. 325–27.

34. TJ to JA, 15 June 1813, ibid., pp. 331–33.

35. JA to TJ, 28 June 1813, ibid., pp. 338–40.

36. JA to TJ, 15 July 1813, ibid., p. 358.

37. TJ to JA, 27 June 1813, ibid., pp. 335–38.

38. JA to TJ, 13 July 1813, ibid., p. 355.

39. TJ to JA, 28 October 1813, ibid., pp. 387–92.

40. JA to TJ, 15 November 1813, ibid., p. 400.

41. The 1814 letters to John Taylor are collected in Adams, ed., *Works*, VI, 445–521.

42. *Journal of Debates and Proceedings in the Convention of Delegates, Chosen to Revise the Constitution of Massachusetts* (Boston, 1853), pp. 277–79.

43. TJ to Samuel Kercheval, 12 July 1816, Ford, ed., *Writings*, X, 37–45.

44. JA to TJ, 15 July 1813, Cappon, ed., *Adams-Jefferson Letters*, p. 358.

45. TJ to Correa de Serra, 23 June 1815, Jefferson Papers Microfilm (Massachusetts Historical Society).

46. TJ to JA, 18 October 1813, 11 January 1816, 4 September 1823, Cappon, ed., *Adams-Jefferson Letters*, pp. 391, 459–60, 596–97.

47. JA to TJ, 16 July 1814, 2 February 1816, ibid., pp. 435, 461.

48. For JA's marginalia, see Haraszti, *Adams and the Prophets of Progress*. See also JA to TJ, 2 March 1816, Cappon, ed., *Adams-Jefferson Letters*, pp. 464–65.

49. JA to TJ, 2 February 1816, ibid., p. 462.

50. JA to TJ, 3 February 1821, ibid., p. 571.

51. TJ to JA, 1 August 1816, also 17 May 1818, 22 January 1821, ibid., pp. 484–85, 524, 570.

52. JA to TJ, 19 May 1821, ibid., p. 572.

53. TJ to JA, 12 September 1821, ibid., p. 575.

54. JA to TJ, 30 July 1815, ibid., p. 451.

55. JA to Benjamin Rush, 4 April 1790, Biddle, ed., *Old Family Letters*, p. 55.

56. JA to Hezekiah Niles, 13 February 1818, Adams, ed., *Works*, X, 283–84.

57. TJ to William Wirt, 4 September 1816, Ford, ed., *Writings*, X, 58–60; JA to Benjamin Waterhouse, 17 August 1817, Ford, ed., *Statesman and Friend*, p. 137.

58. Quoted in Haraszti, *Adams and the Prophets of Progress*, p. 174.

59. The Syllabus is included in TJ to Benjamin Rush, 21 April 1803, Ford, ed., *Writings*, VIII, 223–28.

60. TJ to JA, 12 October 1813, Cappon, ed., *Adams-Jefferson Letters*, pp. 383–86. The "Philosophy of Jesus" led, in turn, to TJ's "Life and Morals of Jesus of Nazareth," which may be found in facsimile in Lipscomb and Bergh, eds., vol. XX.

61. JA to TJ, 16 July 1813, Cappon, ed., *Adams-Jefferson Letters*, p. 360.

62. TJ to Benjamin Rush, 21 April 1803, Ford, ed., *Writings*, VIII, 223n.

63. See JA to TJ, 16 July 1813, Cappon, ed., *Adams-Jefferson Letters*, p. 360.

64. TJ to JA, 19 March 1820, ibid., p. 562.

65. JA to TJ, 18 July 1813, ibid., p. 362.

66. JA to TJ, 4 November 1816, ibid., p. 494.

67. JA to TJ, 19 April 1817, ibid., p. 509.

68. JA to F. A. Van der Kemp, 27 December 1816, Adams, ed., *Works*, X, 234.

69. TJ to JA, 15 August 1820, also 8 January 1825, Cappon, ed., *Adams-Jefferson Letters*, pp. 568, 605–6.

70. TJ to JA, 12 December 1816, ibid., p. 499.

71. TJ to JA, 10 December 1819, ibid., p. 549.

72. TJ to JA, 22 January 1821, ibid., p. 570.

73. JA to TJ, 3 February 1821, ibid., p. 571. Cf. JA to George Clurman and Jacob Lindley, 24 January 1801, Adams, ed., *Works*, IX, 92–93.

74. *Adams-Cunningham Correspondence*, p. X.

75. TJ to JA, 12 October 1823, Cappon, ed., *Adams-Jefferson Letters*, pp. 600–601.

76. JA to TJ, 20 November 1823, ibid., p. 60.

77. TJ to William B. Giles, 26 December 1825, Ford, ed., *Writings*, X, 254–57.

78. JA to John Whitney, 7 June 1826, Adams, ed., *Works*, X, 417.

79. TJ to Roger C. Weightman, 24 June 1826, Ford, ed., *Writings*, X, 391–92.

80. Eighteen of the eulogies may be found in *A Selection of Eulogies Pro-*

*nounced in the Several States, in Honor of Those Illustrious Patriots and Statesmen,
John Adams and Thomas Jefferson* (Hartford, 1826). The above account is drawn
from Merrill D. Peterson, *The Jefferson Image in the American Mind* (New York,
1960), pp. 3–14.

81. JA to Benjamin Rush, 23 March 1809, Schutz and Adair, eds., *Spur to
Fame*, p. 139.

Index